THE ENVIRONMENT
IN THE AGE OF
THE INTERNET

The Environment in the Age of the Internet

Activists, Communication, and the Digital Landscape

Edited by Heike Graf

https://www.openbookpublishers.com

All external links were active on 5/7/2016 unless otherwise stated and have been archived via the Internet Archive Wayback Machine at https://archive.org/web

Updated digital material and resources associated with this volume are available at https://www.openbookpublishers.com/isbn/9781783742431#resources

Every effort has been made to identify and contact copyright holders and any omission or error will be corrected if notification is made to the publisher.

ISBN Paperback: 978-1-78374-243-1
ISBN Hardback: 978-1-78374-244-8
ISBN Digital (PDF): 978-1-78374-245-5
ISBN Digital ebook (epub): 978-1-78374-246-2
ISBN Digital ebook (mobi): 978-1-78374-247-9
DOI: 10.11647/OBP.0096

Cover photo and design by Heidi Couborn, Trees of Co. Cork, Ireland (2010), CC BY 4.0.

All paper used by Open Book Publishers is SFI (Sustainable Forestry Initiative), PEFC (Programme for the Endorsement of Forest Certification Schemes) and Forest Stewardship Council(r)(FSC(r) certified.

Printed in the United Kingdom, United States, and Australia
by Lightning Source for Open Book Publishers (Cambridge, UK)

Contents

Notes on Contributors   ix

Foreword   xiii

1. Introduction   1
   Heike Graf

   Resonance in News Media   4
   About this Volume   7
   References   17

2. The Environment in Disguise: Insurgency and Digital Media   21
   in the Southern Cone
   Virginia Melián

   Background   24
   Digital Media and Protest   26
   The Study   28
   Camouflaged Arguments   30
   User-Generated Content and Mainstream Media   32
   Networking beyond the Digital   34
   Mobile Personal Engagement   37
   Opportunities for Public Debate   40
   Civic Engagement and Media Practice   42
   Conclusion   46
   References   49

3. Exploitation or Preservation? Your Choice! Digital Modes of   53
   Expressing Perceptions of Nature and the Land
   Coppélie Cocq

   Mining Boom, Land Rights, and Perceptions of the   55
   Environment
   YouTube: A Channel for Environmental Activism   56
   Contesting Narratives   63
   Media Logic   65
   Polarisation or Zone of Contact   69
   Conclusions   71
   References   72

4. Natural Ecology Meets Media Ecology: Indigenous Climate   75
   Change Activists' Views on Nature and Media
   Anna Roosvall and Matthew Tegelberg

   Introduction   75
   Defining Traditional Ecological Knowledge   79
   Defining Media Ecology   81
   Method and Material   83
   Analysis   86
   Conclusions   97
   References   101

5. The Culture of Nature: The Environmental Communication   105
   of Gardening Bloggers
   Heike Graf

   Garden Blogs   106
   Environmental Communication from a Systems-Theoretical   108
   Perspective
   Difference-Theoretical Approach   108
   The Role of Topics   112
   Ecology and Gardening in the Mainstream Media   113
   The Topics of Gardening Blogs   116
   Consumption: Developing/Refusing a 'Buyosphere'   117
   Production: Developing Green Gardening   124
   Conclusions   130
   References   133

6. The Militant Media of Neo-Nazi Environmentalism   137
   Madeleine Hurd and Steffen Werther

    NPD Media: Party Websites   140
    Emotions   141
    The NPD and the Environment   145
    The Neo-Nazi World of *Umwelt & Aktiv*   149
    Nature-Oriented Action: A Cure for National Ills   154
    Women, Youth, and Germanic Nature: From *Umwelt* to   156
    Aktion
    References   165

Index   171

Notes on Contributors

Coppélie Cocq (coppelie.cocq@umu.se) is Associate Professor of Sámi Studies at Humlab, Umeå University, Sweden. Her research interests lie in the fields of folkloristics, digital humanities and environmental humanities, with specific focus on storytelling, place-making and revitalisation in Indigenous contexts. Her recent publications include 'Reading Small Data in Indigenous Contexts: Ethical Perspectives', in *Research Methods for Reading Digital Data in the Digital Humanities*, edited by Griffin and Hayler (2016); 'Mobile Technology in Indigenous Landscapes', in *Indigenous People and Mobile Technologies*, edited by Dyson, Grant and Hendriks (2016); and 'Indigenous Voices on the Web: Folksonomies and Endangered Languages' published in the *Journal of American Folklore* in 2015.

Heike Graf (heike.graf@sh.se) is Associate Professor of Media and Communication Studies at Södertörn University, Stockholm. Her research and teaching centre around environmental communication, with specific interest in theory and digital communication. Recent publications include 'From Wasteland to Flower Bed: Ritual in the Website Communication of Urban Activist Gardeners' published in *Culture Unbound: Journal of Current Cultural Research* in 2014 and 'Examining Garden Blogs as a Communication System', published in the *International Journal of Communication* in 2012.

Madeleine Hurd (madeleine.hurd@sh.se) is Associate Professor of Modern History at Södertörn University, Stockholm. Her research has focused on emotions and gender in medialized rituals of spatial belonging in inter-war Germany and in German far-right environmentalism. Recent publications include 'Nature, the Volk, and the Heimat: The Narratives and Practices of the Far Right Ecologist' (co-authored with Steffen Werther), published in *Baltic Worlds* in 2013; 'Contested Masculinities in Inter-War Flensburg', in *Bordering the Baltic: Scandinavian Boundary-drawing Processes, 1900–2000* (2010), which she also edited; and 'Reporting on Civic Rituals: Texts, Performers and Audience', in *Ritual and Media: Interdisciplinary Perspectives*, edited by Brosius and Polit (2010).

Virginia Melián (virginia.melian@lai.su.se) is Assistant Professor of Media Studies and Latin American Studies at Stockholm University. Her research has focused on media and environmental movements in Latin America. Her overview of Swedish Research on Latin America will be published in the forthcoming *Distant Gazes*, edited by Fredrik Uggla.

Anna Roosvall (anna.roosvall@ims.su.se) is Associate Professor of Media Studies (IMS) at Stockholm University. Her research is centred on the nation-globalisation continuum and theories of justice and solidarity in relation to media in four related areas: climate change and indigenous peoples; migration, mobility and the politics of place; world new images; and cultural journalism. She is currently working with Matthew Tegelberg on the book *Media and Transnational Climate Justice: Indigenous Activism and Climate Politics*, which will be published by Peter Lang.

Matthew Tegelberg (mtegel@yorku.ca) is Assistant Professor of Social Science at York University, Canada. His research on cultural tourism, media representations of indigenous peoples and environmental communication has appeared in *Tourist Studies, Triple C: Communication, Capitalism, & Critique, International Communication Gazette*, and in several edited collections. His current work places emphasis on the impact new media technologies and practices are having in these areas of study. He is part of the research network MediaClimate.

Steffen Werther (steffen.werther@sh.se) is Senior Lecturer and Researcher of Historical and Contemporary Studies at Södertörn University in Stockholm. He is interested in German and Scandinavian history, from the nineteenth century to the present day, with a focus on nationalism, racial theory and National Socialist ideology. His doctoral thesis examined the implementation of the SS's Greater Germanic idea in Denmark. His latest publications include: 'Nordic-Germanic Dreams and National Realities: A Case Study of the Danish Region of Sønderjylland, 1933–1945', in *Racial Science in Hitler's New Europe*, edited by Anton Weiss-Wendt and Rory Yeomans (2013); and 'Go East, Old Man: Space, Ritual and the Politics of Memory among Europe's Waffen-SS Veterans' (co-authored with Madeline Hurd), published in *Culture Unbound* in 2014.

Foreword

The Environment in the Age of the Internet is the result of interdisciplinary cooperation involving research from media and communication studies, social sciences, modern history, and folklore studies. Its focus is on different groups' communicative approaches to ecological issues, with the intent of shedding light on how these groups tell their own stories of 'the' environment.

This book is the culmination of our joint research project 'Communication, and the Social Performance of Environmentalism', funded between 2010–2012 by the Foundation for Baltic and East European Studies at Södertörn University in Sweden. At the start of the project, we were three humanists who analysed the environmental communication of activists, 'ordinary' people, and eco-nationalists. This approach worked towards an understanding of how humans conceptualise and communicate about nature; how they can be motivated, collectively, to act; and what contexts might influence their communication. In this project, we were mostly focused on two culturally related Baltic Sea countries: Sweden and Germany.

However, in this final version of our work, we have gone beyond the Baltic Sea region, broadening the scope of our investigation to include a scholar whose research is on environmental activists in South America. We also include scholars who contribute the perspectives of indigenous people of North America and Northern Europe, further widening our focus to different communication fora and responses to ecological issues.

I would like to thank the Foundation for Baltic and East European Studies (http://ostersjostiftelsen.se/in-english) for the funding that has made the project and this book possible. I would also like to thank

Pamela Marston, Madeleine Hurd, and Steen Christensen for copy-editing the text. Last but not least, I wish to express my gratitude to the anonymous referees for their useful comments on the manuscript, and to the publisher, Open Book Publishers, and its Managing Director Dr. Alessandra Tosi, for their invaluable support of our manuscript.

Heike Graf
Stockholm, April 2016

1. Introduction

Heike Graf

This volume is situated at the intersection of communication, environment, and media. Communication here is not understood as the pure exchange of information, or as dialogue, but instead in a more general sense, as the core element that constitutes society. Without communicating about our environment, meaning here especially the non-human environment, we have no knowledge about dangers such as climate change, pollution, deforestation, etc., and therefore cannot react to them. German sociologist Niklas Luhmann expressed the importance of communication as follows: 'Fish may die, or human beings swimming in lakes and rivers may cause illnesses, no more oil may come from the pumps, and average temperatures may rise or fall, but as long as this is not communicated it does not have any effect on society' (Luhmann 1989, 28–29). In other words, the non-human environment, nature, and the climate, etc., can only be a subject of social concern when it is communicated. And '[e]verything that can be formulated linguistically can be communicated' (Luhmann 1989, 16).

As the environment cannot speak itself or for itself, and, in the words of Robert Cox, 'nature is silent' (2013, 4), it has no possibility of communicating with society. The environment does not contain information or topics. It does not understand our speech, either. It cannot announce itself in terms of issues, saying, for example, that the climate will change. It can only irritate and disturb society by changing temperatures, melting glaciers, and so forth; disturbances which then receive public attention and become public and political concerns.

 http://dx.doi.org/10.11647/OBP.0096.01

In this way, the non-human environment can be seen as an actor influencing communication in society, or in the words of Bruno Latour, as an agent of 'our common geostory' (2014, 3). How to tackle these disturbances is the subject of social communication, where someone 'makes claims (in public) about them' (Hansen 2010, 15) and, in other words, tells 'stories'. Stories about ecological dangers and risks can be described as an attribution process, that is, as a construction of an observer (an individual person or a social system) about the 'possibility of future damage' (Luhmann 1990, 225). 'The problem becomes for all of us in philosophy, science or literature, *how* do we tell such a story' (Latour 2014, 3, my emphasis). Or, in the words of Luhmann: 'the whole problem thereby becomes an internal problem of modern society' (Luhmann 1996, 6).

Stories are told within a context; examining the 'what' and 'how' of these environmental stories demonstrates how contexts condition communication. These contexts affect what is said, written, and shown. Without these contexts, meaningful communication would not be possible. Still, even a carefully designed message cannot control its outcome, and therefore does not guarantee consensus or agreement with the message.

The message as a kind of constraint enacted by communication always makes different understandings possible (Luhmann 1996). One may, for instance, expect that the picture of a charismatic mega fauna has a greater emotional impact than the features of an insect. However, it depends on the observer, and on the context of the message being observed. If we apply constructivist theories, the act of understanding allows for different ways of proceeding, because understanding is not predetermined by the message but instead relates to the observer/person who perceives it. The observer constructs meaning on the basis of what he or she is able to see and feel. Or, in the words of Stuart Hall: 'we give them [things] a meaning' through a 'framework of interpretation' (Hall 1997, 3). The image as such does not contain 'any fixed and unchanging meaning' (Hall 1997, 3). Hence, it is not the image that determines the meaning production, but the observer. Here again, the observer perspective is crucial when analysing communication processes. How else would it be possible to explain that there are persons who are more fascinated by insects than by charismatic fauna? The picture creates some restrictive conditions, but cannot ultimately control how it is understood, and cannot control emotional responses. There is no causal link between the image and its effect (Bateson 1979).

We return to the relationship between the non-human environment and society by focusing on the concept of communication. This does not contradict indigenous approaches in which nature can only speak to those who listen, in order to know what is going on (e.g., Carbaugh 1999). Nature can, of course, be experienced by individuals as something with a voice. However, without further communicating what has been heard, nature stays in observers' minds and cannot become a topic of social communication. What is central to this approach is that communication is understood as a social operation with at least two persons involved.

Therefore, society is 'prevented' from directly communicating with the environment, and can only communicate about it or 'tell stories', even if voices claim to speak for the environment. Epistemologically, a story of Gaia cannot be equated with nature. It is a story *about* nature. Consequently, there are as many stories as there are persons telling them.

The above-mentioned distinction between society and the non-human environment should not be confused with a hierarchal distinction that values one side over the other, as criticised in ecocritical studies (Urry 2011). It is not about a division that places society on one side and nature as the external environment on the other without any correlation. This distinction has to be understood as a cognitive one, which according to observation theories (Schutz 2011; von Foerster 1960/1984; Maturana and Varela 1987) means that our point of departure is communication. Observing means to make an indication in the context of a distinction. We claim, for instance, that this last winter was warmer than the winter before. We first distinguish winter from other seasons, and then indicate the winter side of the distinction. Observing as an operation means 'using a distinction for indicating one side of the distinction and not the other' (Luhmann 1993, 485). If we do not make any distinctions, we cannot claim anything. Consequently, making a distinction between humans and nature does not *per se* imply seeing nature as something subordinated or separated. According to observation theories, we cannot indicate the 'human' side of the distinction without keeping it distinct from something which is not 'human'. So, every observation carries with it the other side of the distinction, meaning what is not indicated. Here, the notion of humans carries with it the notion of nature. The approach of drawing distinctions is seen as a basic, cognitive operation of communication as such.

This approach of phenomenology does not compete with ecocritics, as they have another point of departure. Ecocritics see the distinction between society and nature as a normative and hierarchical one. They already look at what kind of indications are made; they criticize 'the colonial dominance of European philosophical traditions' (Rust et al. 2016, 2) where the environment is seen as something to conquer. Humans have subdued and controlled the non-human environment for their own needs without considering the consequences. Human progress is seen in terms of society's exploitation of nature (Urry 2011). Consequently, humans are divided from nature, a division that is questioned by ecocritics who say that society cannot exist without nature. Therefore, they demand 'new frames of references and the ability to reframe familiar media frames' (Rust et al. 2016, 5).

Here, the points of departure are on different levels, with the first one based on observers' cognition and the latter on patterns of communication, e.g., on indications made by observers (European philosophers, media, activists etc.). By looking further at what kinds of claims are made, and at what kinds of distinctions they are based on, we can see how the relationship between humans and nature is constructed. This operation of analysis is also based on distinctions that can be either descriptive or normative. The consequence of this communicative approach is that it draws focus to the observer making claims about the environment, and prompts us to examine who this observer is: a theoretical perspective that relates to the phenomenologist Alfred Schutz (2011).

Resonance in News Media

Since the environment does not announce itself in the media, there has to be someone who can linguistically formulate environmental issues, and therefore begin communicating about them. Whatever we know about the environment, both non-human and human, we know from the (mass) media (Luhmann 1996, 4). Or more metaphorically, in the words of Mark Deuze: 'Media are to us as water is to fish' (2012, x). So, media play the central role in constructing and spreading communication about environmental issues in order for them to be recognised as public or political concerns.

Luhmann defines the relationship between the environment and society, as well as that between the environment and media, through the concept of resonance (Luhmann 1989). Strictly speaking, this concept is contrary to the traditional realist notion of media as a mirror of reality or to the notion of news media as 'windows' on the world (Hansen 2010, 17). It is similar to the lived-body and consciousness: our body has no direct communicative channel to our consciousness, telling us, for instance, what is wrong when it hurts. Instead it irritates us with feelings of pain, pressure, etc. (Luhmann 1989, 29).

This concept of resonance refers to constructivist approaches which claim that our picture of the world depends on who is doing the observing. If we look at media organisations as the observer, we claim that they can only observe what is going on in the environment on the basis of their internal operations, and this is related, for example, to issues of media logic (Altheide 2013).

Not everything can be said, written about, or spread through the media; selection must be made and based on a 'very restricted resonance capacity' (Luhmann 1989, 17) of each medium or even communication forum, finally resulting in a media-specific description of the natural environment. In the words of Latour: '[…] journalists are journalists, mere storytellers, just like novelists; you know how they are: they always feel obliged to add some action to what, in essence, should be devoid of any form of will, goal, target, or obsession. Even when they are interested in science and nature, they can't help but add drama to what has no drama whatsoever' (Latour 2014, 11).

Hence, the purpose of this volume is to investigate the ways in which the environment finds resonance in different communication forums, understood as observers in the sense described above. Of particular interest to us is to look at how different communication forums respond to the environment and therefore reveal their own conceptions, their own stories of 'the' environment by using different media devices and formats. Environmental concerns are packaged, narrated (Labov and Waletzky 1967), or framed (Entman 1993) according to the observers' or group's own operations. Understanding these contexts can assist in showing how specific environmental issues arise. In other words, this volume is about how humans engage with each other in the context of their own operations and the environment, including the media environment they are situated in. We assume that communication about nature affects the way we engage with the non-human environment.

If we look at how the environment finds resonance in traditional mass media, we discover a bulk of research. In this respect, most media research is about media coverage, that is, about how media portray the non-human environment (e.g., Hansen 1993; Lester 2010). The media introduce their own means of grasping natural events, and these events appear to them as information. Media observation of the environment is highly selective, and certain distinctions that can be described as having news value (novelty, proximity, scandals, norm violations, conflicts, quantities, etc.) guide the news production process (see e.g., Boykoff and Boykoff 2007).

We know from research that news media mainly create their own preferred meanings of environmental issues by tackling them as problems and dangers (e.g., Cox 2013; Foust and O'Shannon Murphy 2009). News coverage prefers conflict, and with the help of the rhetoric of fear or what Altheide calls 'production of fear' (Altheide 1997), we as media consumers learn that something is wrong with our environment and that we are faced with risks and dangers. For example, environmental stories are unlike other science stories, as they are mainly 'marked by negativity' (Einsiedel and Coughland 1993; Olausson 2009) and told in a 'fear-generating' manner. These stories are about an 'uncontrollable nature' that poses risks to people, made vivid by the use of attention-getting words and phrases such as 'disastrous effects', 'increased mortality', 'diseases', 'treacherous bacteria', 'catastrophe', and 'accidents'. These 'establish the negative and frightful context in which climate change is discursively constructed' (Olausson 2009, 11). According to a survey of U.S. mainstream news media's coverage of risk (Lundgren and McMakin, 2009), 'mass media disproportionately focus on hazards that are catastrophic and violent in nature. [...] Drama, symbolism, and identifiable victims, particularly children and celebrities, make risks more memorable' (cit. in Cox 2013, 168). Global climate change, for instance, is covered as 'something to collectively fear', and if we do not behave in a climate-friendly way, 'we should feel guilt' (Höijer 2010, 727). In sum, the term environment itself is associated with problems in news media (Hansen 2010, 1). As a result, scholars complain that complex environmental issues are packaged as simplistic and dramatised (Cox 2013). What appears in the media as the reality of nature is simply the product of media production that emphasises certain things and de-emphasises others.

Fear-related communication can be understood as a principle of resonance (Luhmann 1989). Such communication states the worst and is therefore infused with morality in its explanations of what is good and bad for society and the non-human environment. Fear is an attractive and universal rhetoric when it comes to justifying moral judgments. It becomes almost a duty to worry about our natural environment; one can expect that others share our worries, and one has the right to demand changes (Luhmann 1989, 161).

This journalistic tactic nevertheless has an impact on our relationship to the environment. The massive amount of negative and problem-oriented news reports about our physical environment (air, water, food) promotes a sense of numerous crises and risks. The fear frame does not allow for arguments that any progress has been made concerning environmental issues. 'As such news media can foster public anxiety about issues that scientists find less worrisome' (Cox and Pezullio 2016, 167).

About this Volume

However, mass media organisations are not the only ones who communicate about the environment in public; there are also other actors. In this volume, humanities scholars and social scientists analyse the communication of different actors who more or less claim to create awareness of the non-human environment. This volume contains research on communities formed by environmental activists, including a grassroots organisation based in Argentina and two environmental NGOs in Uruguay who led protests against the construction of pulp mills on the banks of the Uruguay River and against monoculture forestry in their country (Melían). It also touches on the local people of Sápmi, the traditional area of settlement of the indigenous people of northern

Europe, who have made their voices heard against the growing mining industry in northern Sweden (Cocq). This book also discusses activists from indigenous organisations that represent natural ecosystems from across the globe and seek to shape public opinion on the effects of climate change on indigenous lands (Roosvall and Tegelberg). This volume contains research on a mixture of non-traditional environmental groups: 'ordinary' people in Sweden and Germany who blog about their hobby, gardening, and argue for more or less ecological behaviour in the garden (Graf), and neo-Nazi environmentalists in Germany who use ecological engagement to increase their movements' visibility and to project a positive image (Hurd and Werther).

Media

Generally, we have to admit that the communication forums examined are situated in a (post) modern media environment characterised by information overload (Andrejevic 2013) or by a surplus of meaning and 'the culture of dealing with this surplus selectively' (Baecker 2011, 5). These media-saturated contexts are especially challenging for marginalised groups who want to make their voices heard. We are particularly interested in how different types of communication media create different discursive fields and performances in a mediatised society. Or, in the words of Luhmann (Luhmann 1989), how the environment finds resonance and is communicated by different groups.

Media comes into play in different ways for all of the above-mentioned groups. Activists in Argentina and Uruguay used digital media, especially websites, newsletters, e-mails, and mobile phones, in their articulation, dissemination, and organisation of environmental protest actions (Melián). That was years ago: social media have now become the main means of harnessing attention for, e.g., the concerns of local people in the Sápmi area (Cocq). Blogging is used by 'ordinary' people in order to spread opinions and experiences regarding gardening (Graf). In addition to the face-to-face world of direct action, neo-Nazis spread their ecological messages via party websites and quarterly magazines (Hurd and Werther).

The use of different media as well the perspectives of the producers of information have an impact on a group and its organisation (see

Bennett and Segerberg 2013) in addition to what is being communicated. This volume also includes a text focusing on activists working for indigenous perspectives on climate change. These activists reflect on the impact of the different media landscapes — national, mainstream, local, alternative, and non-/indigenous — that they are confronted with, and on how they develop strategies to overcome the marginalisation of their voices (Roosvall and Tegelberg). The activists speak of a national news ecology which rarely makes room for indigenous perspectives or knowledge of nature. Hence, indigenous people's own media practices attempt to generate awareness of these issues in the public sphere, which, of course, influences the way their messages are framed. The mainstream media are still seen as the most powerful vehicle for increasing awareness and are, therefore, addressed accordingly. Mainstream media remain a powerful source of meaning production. In the case of a garden blogger, the growing number of TV programs and magazines on gardening affect how a garden is perceived and how it is communicated in the blog community. It has been considered common sense to prioritise sustainable gardening, to work towards increasing biodiversity, to attempt to conserve natural resources, etc. This may explain why communication about damaging the environment, by using chemicals for example, is almost absent (Graf).

Of course, the different media formats influence the 'how' and the 'what' of environmental communication. Various media employ more-or-less strict forms of how things can be said or visualised. Newspapers follow certain ritualised narrative forms. In social media, a blog group makes use of blog entries and replies by referring to traditional media; for instance, a video clip is based on narratives from motion pictures. Media converge and overlap, from the traditional newspaper to the social media forum of the Internet (Jenkins 2006). Digital formats can be easily shared by an audience that is, in our case, receptive to arguments about sustainability, environmental preservation, the traditional use of natural resources, and respect for the natural and cultural landscape as described by Coppélie Cocq.

We do not mean that these different media formats simply determine how the message is expressed, but instead see them as conditioning factors. To put it differently, media technologies condition what is possible in concrete media practices, that is, the construction of a message in some way. For instance, as Cocq notes, the format of a short video in participatory media requires a degree of message simplification if one wants to reach out. The same goes for the other communication forums. A website also demands simplification, as does a blog post. In other words, media formats generally enforce selectivity, which in turn leads to a reduction of complexity.

The reduction of complexity is also related to the imagined target group. If one wants to attract the mass media, one tries to adopt media logic. When one makes use of news values, for instance, by playing up a story's sensationalism, then the aim is to receive attention from the mass media, a process described by Anna Roosvall and Matthew Tegelberg. If instead the target group is one's own blog community or political community, one then follows the communicative rules and common understandings of this group to connect, as shown in both Heike Graf's and Madeleine Hurd and Steffen Werther's chapters.

Technological conditions also apply. Given the fact that smartphones were not available at the time of the protest actions against the construction of pulp mills in Latin America, activists did not exclusively use the Internet to organise the protest or directly disseminate information. As Virginia Melían notes, the dissemination of information had to be both digital and analogue to overcome the digital divide in this region. However, the Internet was extensively used for establishing an organisational infrastructure composed of different environmental groups, and was also a source for retrieving information and spreading alternative discourses which otherwise had difficulty entering the public sphere. Often, the content of emails and newsletters were printed out and distributed among people at meetings, and local radio stations also broadcast information about the protest.

The chapter by Roosvall and Tegelberg broadens our perspective by looking at 'media ecology' as bounded by nation states. 'Ecology' in this sense means the entire media technology landscape in which indigenous actors are situated. Since it is still dominated by mainstream media, which rarely make use of indigenous perspectives, especially when it comes to traditional ecological knowledge, indigenous actors have limited access to the types of communication required to reach a larger audience. Here, we can also speak of a form of media divide, in which indigenous actors are restricted to social media platforms to disseminate their own messages. The authors argue that this media imbalance requires a reshaping of the current media ecology to address climate change issues from a broader perspective, one which includes traditional ecological knowledge.

The way in which the non-human environment finds resonance in different communication forums relates not only to the non-human and media environment but also to the political environment. For example, in the case of the protest actions in Latin America, activists' choice of arguments was greatly affected by the ruling left-wing coalition in Uruguay. These activists carefully selected their arguments to avoid being cut off from communication (Melían).

Does communication matter? Examining the impact of communication, and following the communicative approach detailed above, demonstrates that communication succeeds first of all when connections can be established, and then again when recipients take the communicated information as a premise for their own actions and meaning production. There are two cases in this volume where such impact can be noted. In the case of the resistance against mining companies in the Sápmi area, less than two years after the publication of the first YouTube videos discussed in the chapter, the topic has shifted from the periphery to the centre of the public debate (Cocq). The environmental protest actions on the banks of the Uruguay River, which took place between 2005 and 2009, are now considered turning points in the public and political awareness of environmental issues, due to increased mass media attention (Melían).

Frames of Communication

We are interested in exploring how different groups react to ecological issues, and how they package their messages: what kinds of topics or types of approaches are used to create awareness and receive attention in the present media environment? Themes have to be adjusted to the groups' conditions of communicability. They are 'framed', meaning according to Robert Entman, 'to select some aspects of a perceived reality and make them more salient in a communicating text' (1993, 52). The examples included in our volume allow us to identify the following frames of communication.

Against the backdrop of a political situation in which environmental issues are downplayed and seen as luxury problems by political elites, environmental activists in Argentina and Uruguay initiated spectacular events in order to receive media attention (Melían). Information about their eye-catching actions was sent directly to mainstream media journalists via mobile phones, for instance, in order to interest them in covering the events. The news values selected here were those of oddity and drama. On activists' websites, environmental concerns were framed as political and economic concerns by highlighting the risks of pulp mills, rather than as purely environmental issues. By making use of news values such as consequence and proximity through highlighting the risks, and by topically connecting the environment issue to ongoing political discourse, the actions attracted a high level of media attention. Using mostly the frames of danger and risk, these groups finally received attention from mainstream media as well as from politicians.

In the case of YouTube video clips produced by the activists aiming to direct national and international attention to the Sápmi area, the frames used are those of disrupted harmony, conflict, and uncertainty (Cocq). Images of indigenous people's respect for the natural and cultural landscape are contrasted with images of devastation and destruction wrought by the mining industry. Proximity (as a news value) is also employed. The viewer is involved in the story by being asked 'What is YOUR choice? Take a stand!', and by being offered a solution to the conflict, namely 'join the movement'. The mode of communication is borrowed from (advertising) media and is therefore familiar and recognisable in terms of language and framing. As a result, the mining boom on indigenous land has received greater attention in Swedish public debate.

The same goes for indigenous peoples' voices in the ongoing debate over climate change. Their voices are barely heard in mainstream media, despite the population's extensive experiences with environmental issues (Roosvall and Tegerberg). Their media practices consist of an active presence on social media platforms in order to document and share indigenous knowledge about nature. Since the impact of these alternative channels is limited, the activists also seek mainstream media attention by making use of media's news values. For example, by selecting values of proximity and consequence, dangers relating to community health risks are highlighted. By engaging celebrities, their information is given prominence and novelty. The exoticism card is also played: at public events such as demonstrations and press gatherings, many indigenous activists wear traditional clothing in order to stand out and direct attention to cultural identity issues.

In the case of gardening blogs, ecological topics have to be adjusted to themes of garden life (Graf). This implies that if one wants to be part of this blogosphere and intends to trigger connecting communication in the form of comments and 'likes', one should include ecological concerns, such as global warming, as part of gardening issue content. For example, climate change as such is not discussed but, in relation to dryness, it can be connected to methods for keeping the soil moist for longer periods. In other words, communication is framed in such a way that blog entries are constantly coordinated with each other. These frames conform to the norms of the examined blogosphere with respect to subject matter and the manner of communication. The author concludes that gardening issues are characterised by frames of pleasure, enthusiasm, and mutual agreement. These blog networks establish a kind of feel-good atmosphere that stands in stark contrast to the apocalyptic rhetoric of the news media's coverage of environmental issues.

In contrast to the above mentioned community, the online communication of neo-Nazis is 'brisk and angry in tone' (Hurd and Werther); environmentalism is placed within xenophobic arguments by propagating a German 'biomass' ideology as an 'argument for territorial exclusiveness'. By highlighting distinctions of proximity and consequence, what is implied is that German landscapes are indissolubly connected to German culture, which is in danger from invasive human and animal immigrants. In line with this militant environmentalism, ecological messages are mainly framed as threats against the German people and culture. For example, genetically manipulated foods and low-wage food imports are presented as harming local production. Nature is integrated into the human condition primarily by using the rhetoric of fear as well as those of nostalgia and love. In the long run, ecological arguments work to gain acceptance for xenophobic ideologies in society. As this chapter shows, environmental communication can be marshalled to promote xenophobic ideas.

In sum, it is striking to note how necessary it is to adapt media logic, as in the selected frames of communication, to acquire public attention. This illustrates mediatisation theories (e.g., Hjarvard 2013), which claim that the logic of media institutions condition how messages are communicated. Journalistic news values are used, including negativity, oddity, proximity, consequence, and prominence. Conflicts are the focal points: environmentalists versus politicians and companies, indigenous knowledge versus mainstream knowledge, nature versus society, idyllic *Heimat* versus global capital, and so forth.

This volume also shows that the frequent use of the rhetorical strategies of fear and threats is not limited to news media communication, but also belongs to the common repertoire of rhetorical strategies employed by activists, environmentalists, and ideologists. By primarily using frames of danger and risk, their emphasis is placed on worst-case scenarios, which can evoke emotions of fear, anxiety, and anger. Environmental movements use these frames in order to influence attitudes and promote the adoption of environmentally-conscious roles, while political movements use them to attract supporters. However, if the aim is not to persuade people and merely to communicate about a hobby such as gardening, ecological issues are framed in a positive and enjoyable manner. If conflicts arise, they have to be addressed in an ironic tone in order to follow the normative rules of garden blog communication. In sum, the communication preferences, aims, contexts, etc. all condition the way in which things are said, written, and shown.

Even if we are all more or less worried about climate change or other ecological issues, communication forums base these issues on their own preferences and purposes. Some voices are more prominent in public than others. Indigenous people might view nature as sacred based on their traditional ecological knowledge. Activists base their environmental protests on the attempt to protect nature by preventing and stopping the exploitation of natural resources. Gardeners might label nature, the garden, as a commodity they can enjoy. Neo-Nazis might see nature as an idyll they are willing to fight for with militant xenophobia.

Here, we can isolate some of the fundamental problems of communication about ecological issues in society. We see different meanings about the non-human environment constructed in these cases.

All the groups covered in this volume communicate in different ways when articulating the problem and elaborating on possible solutions. The non-human environment can be addressed from all conceivable angles. Nature is everywhere, but is observed differently. For example, when the Spanish slug invades gardens, the advice given is to kill them. When the mining industry devastates indigenous land, one is asked to join the protest movement. When the *Heimat* is changing, you have to stop immigration of all kinds.

We all refer to different things when we speak about the non-human environment as we approach the non-human environment from different angles. The news media treat ecological issues from the perspective of what is newsworthy or even entertaining. The tiny blog community looks at matters from the vantage of what is enjoyable. Politicians as well as activists approach the issues from the angle of power over decisions, while business and economic interests approach these issues from the point of view of economic value. And if we look at scholars, their point of departure is from what is scientifically verifiable (Luhmann 1989). These different perspectives (or communication systems) complicate successful communication about ecological issues, since we have to consider that every observation has structural limits. Such complication also applies to any kind of scientific observation of nature. Hence the problem of social communication as such, which is that of acquiring different kind of insights (Luhmann 1989).

Scholars claim that a 'new vision' (Corbett 2006, 307) able to combine all of the different insights is required to change human behaviour. On the one hand, theoretically, it would be difficult to establish a new vision, or a new morality, in a modern and highly-differentiated society that makes use of varied social systems and agendas in addressing environmental concerns. No one element, be it political or economic, can claim to represent society holistically. There is therefore no single counterpart to the non-human environment. However, the more differentiated a society is, the more likely it is to produce resonance and continue to develop (Luhmann 1989, 15). On the other hand, if we look at it empirically, it seems that in the public sphere the frequently used frame of fear and anxiety has led to a new style of morality in our society. This new style is based on a common interest in the alleviation of fear and anxiety; that is, so that people can live without either. The fear and anxiety frame is universal and, hence, can be used in all contexts. Moreover, the communication of fear and anxiety is always authentic; speaking of suffering from fear and anxiety 'resists any kind of critique' (Luhmann 1989, 128). No one who addresses the fear of climate change or, more concretely, the fear of genetically modified food appears in a negative light. Fear as such cannot be forbidden or falsified by scholars; it is just there. Hence, it cannot be contested in social communication. Communicating about the environment from this kind of emotional vantage point, it is unclear how the relationship between society and the non-human environment can be improved. Only the future can show whether fear and anxiety have been justified (Luhmann 1989).

References

Altheide, David L., 'The News Media, the Problem Frame, and the Production of Fear', *The Sociological Quarterly*, 38(4) (Autumn 1997), 647–668, http://dx.doi.org/10.1111/j.1533-8525.1997.tb00758.x

—, 'Media Logic, Social Control, and Fear', *Communication Theory*, 23(3) (2013), 223–238, http://dx.doi.org/10.1111/comt.12017

Andrejevic, Mark, *Infoglut: How too Much Information is Changing the Way We Think and Know* (New York and London: Routledge, 2013), http://dx.doi.org/10.4324/9780203075319

Bateson, Gregory, *Mind and Nature. A Necessary Unity* (New York: Dutton, 1979).

Baecker, Dirk, 'What Is Holding Societies Together? On Culture Forms, World Models, and Concepts of Time', *Criticism*, 53(1) (2011), 1–22, http://dx.doi.org/10.1353/crt.2011.0004

Boykoff, Maxwell T. and Boykoff, Jules M., 'Climate Change and Journalistic Norms: A Case-Study of US Mass-Media Coverage', *Geoforum*, 38(6) (2007), 1190–1204, http://dx.doi.org/10.1016/j.geoforum.2007.01.008

Bennett, Lance and Segerberg, Alexandra, *The Logic of Connective Action. Digital Media and the Personalization of Continuous Politics* (Cambridge: Cambridge University Press, 2013), http://dx.doi.org/10.1017/cbo9781139198752.004

Carbaugh, Donal, 'Just Listen: "Listening" and Landscape among the Blackfeet', *Western Journal of Communication*, 63(3) (1999), 250–270, http://dx.doi.org/10.1080/10570319909374641

Corbett, Julia B., *Communicating Nature. How We Create and Understand Environmental Messages* (Washington: Island Press, 2006).

Cox, J. Robert, *Environmental Communication and the Public Sphere* (Thousand Oaks: Sage, 2013).

—, and Pezzulio, Phaedra C., *Environmental Communication and the Public Sphere* (Thousand Oaks: Sage, 2016).

Deuze, Mark, *Media Life* (Cambridge: Polity, 2012), http://dx.doi.org/10.1177/0163443710386518

Einsiedel, Edna F. and Coughlan, Eileen, 'The Canadian Press and the Environment: Reconstructing a Social Reality', in *The Mass Media and Environmental Issues*, ed. by Andreas Hansen (Leicester: Leicester University Press, 1993), pp. 134–149.

Entman, Robert M., 'Framing: Towards Clarification of a Fractured Paradigm', *Journal of Communication*, 4 (1993), 51–58, http://dx.doi.org/10.1111/j.1460-2466.1993.tb01304.x

Foust, Christina R. and O'Shannon Murphy, William, 'Revealing and Reframing Apocalyptic Tragedy in Global Warming Discourse', *Environmental Communication: A Journal of Nature and Culture*, 3(2) (2009), 151–167, http://dx.doi.org/10.1080/17524030902916624

Hall, Stuart, ed., *Representation: Cultural Representations and Signifying Practices* (London: Sage, 1997).

Hansen, Andreas, ed., *The Mass Media and Environmental Issues* (Leicester: Leicester University Press, 1993).

—, *Environment, Media and Communication* (New York: Routledge, 2010), http://dx.doi.org/10.4324/9780203860014

Hjavard, Stig, *The Mediatization of Culture and Society* (London: Routledge, 2013).

Höijer, Birgitta, 'Emotional Anchoring and Objectification in the Media Reporting on Climate Change', *Public Understanding of Science*, 19 (2010), 717–731, http://dx.doi.org/10.1177/0963662509348863

Jenkins, Henry, *Convergence Culture: Where Old and New Media Collide* (New York: New York University Press, 2006).

Labov, William and Waletzky, Joshua, 'Narrative Analysis', in *Essays on the Verbal and Visual Arts*, ed. by June Helm (Seattle: University of Washington Press, 1967), pp. 12–44.

Latour, Bruno, 'Agency at the Time of the Anthropocene', *New Literary History*, 45(1) (2014), 1–18, http://dx.doi.org/10.1353/nlh.2014.0003

Lester, Libby, *Media and Environment: Conflict, Politics and the News* (Cambridge: Polity, 2010).

Luhmann, Niklas, *Ecological Communication* (Chicago: University of Chicago Press, 1989).

—, 'Technology, Environment and Social Risk: A Systems Perspective', *Industrial Crisis Quarterly* 4 (1990), 223–231.

—, 'Observing Re-entries', *Graduate Faculty Philosophy Journal*, 16(2) (1993), 485–498, http://dx.doi.org/10.5840/gfpj199316227

—, *Die Realität der Massenmedien* (Opladen: Westdeutscher Verlag, 1996), http://dx.doi.org/10.1007/978-3-663-01103-3

Lundgren, Regina E. and McMakin, Andrea H., *Risk Communication. A Handbook for Communicating Environmental Safety, and Health Risks* (Hoboken, NJ: John Wiley, 2009).

Maturana, Humberto R. and Varela, Francisco J., *The Tree of Knowledge: The Biological Roots of Human Understanding* (Boston: Shambhala, 1987).

Olausson, Ulrika, 'Global Warming — Global Responsibility? Media Frames of Collective Action and Scientific Certainty', *Public Understanding of Science*, 18(4) (2009), 421–436, http://dx.doi.org/10.1177/0963662507081242

Rust, Stephen, Monani, Salma and Cubitt, Sean, 'Introduction', in *Ecomedia: Key Issues*, ed. by Stephen Rust, Salma Monani and Sean Cubitt (London and New York: Routledge, 2016), http://dx.doi.org/10.4324/9781315769820

Schutz, Alfred, *Collected Papers V. Phenomenology and the Social Sciences*, ed. by Lester Embree (Dordrecht, Heidelberg, London and New York: Springer, 2011), http://dx.doi.org/10.1007/978-94-007-1515-8

Urry, John, *Climate Change and Society* (Cambridge: Polity, 2011).

Von Foerster, Heinz, *Observing Systems* (Seaside: Intersystems Publications, 1984 [1960]).

2. The Environment in Disguise: Insurgency and Digital Media in the Southern Cone

Virginia Melián

During the last few decades, a growing awareness of the consequences of human activity on the environment and an intense debate about environmental risks and the threat posed by civilization have become evident in Western societies. This has been stressed by, for example, Ulrich Beck (1992) and Manuel Castells (2000). In Latin America, however, environmental concerns have remained barely visible. Civil society organisations and social movements struggle to bring to the fore their concerns about the risks that increasing pollution poses to the ecosystem and the life of local communities. Political elites generally downplay environmental concerns, arguing that these are 'luxury problems', typical of some industrialized countries but hardly relevant in the context of developing societies, since the latter must exploit their natural resources in order to provide social welfare for their citizens. Environmental norms are generally weak in the region. Lack of attention on part of the established political parties has contributed to a lack of mainstream, journalistic coverage, since the media give preference to issues prioritised by political and economic powers, rather than those that concern the civil society (as has been pointed out by Waisbord 2000; Hallin and Papathanassopoulos 2002; Fox and Waisbord 2002 and Rockwell and Janus 2003). For instance, a recent study on the space given to mobilisations in the main national newspapers of 17 Latin American

 http://dx.doi.org/10.11647/OBP.0096.02

countries reveals that less than 15% of the total number of protests covered between 2009 and 2010 were focused on environmental issues (Calderón 2012).

Despite scant media coverage, inadequate environmental policies, and a lack of political interest, recent protests organised by citizens' groups and various NGOs based in different countries demonstrate that the continent is far from unconcerned about the environment. In several cases, civic engagement has been organised in response to industrial pollution that affects protected or untouched areas, citizens' living conditions and the future of flora and fauna, as documented by Jussi Pakkasvirta (2008), Silvio Waisbord and Enrique Peruzzoti (2009) and Yanina Welp and Jonathan Wheatly (2012). In many cases, the citizens' concern focuses on the exploitation of natural resources, often by polluting industries that move to the South to avoid stringent regulations in their countries of origin (FAO 2009, 77). This upsurge in civil society engagement, in general, occurs in the context of Latin America's so-called third wave of democratisation, which is characterised by a significant increase in civic activity in post-authoritarian nations (Avritzer 2002, 3). The rising number of Latin-American environmental protests over the last few years, and the rapidly changing conditions of the continent's media landscape caused by citizens' increasing access to the Internet and mobile phones, raise questions about the role played by digital media in organisation and mobilisation, dissemination of information, formulation of arguments and facilitation of public debate.

In this chapter, I analyse how digital media were used for the formulation, dissemination and organisation of an environmental protest action against the construction of pulp mills on the banks of the Uruguay River and against monoculture forestry in Uruguay. Three different groups, one grassroots organisation based in Argentina and two environmental NGOs in Uruguay, led the protests from 2005 until 2009. Special focus is placed on the ways in which arguments behind the protest were formulated. This protest movement — and in particular the Argentinean grassroots group component — has been seen as a turning point in the historical trajectory of environmental movements, according to Waisbord and Peruzzotti (2009), both because of the large number of people involved and because of the media attention it managed to receive. The results presented here are based on my doctoral thesis, completed in September 2012 at Stockholm University.

This case study offers an opportunity to examine the interplay between digital media and environmental protest in a non-Western context. The organisations studied are based in countries that are comparable in terms of Internet usage and demographics. The period under consideration, 2005–2009, is likewise significant because it coincides with the initial expansion of digital media in these countries. The case also represents an historical turning point because levels of Internet and mobile phone access expanded greatly in Latin America during and after this period. Over the last years, the advancement of social media platforms and smart phones has made new kinds of digital media available. Young people organised in new constellations of spontaneous groups increasingly use several networking opportunities embedded in social media and smart phones (compared to newsletters, e-mail and SMS used initially). For instance, social media played a prominent role during the so called 'Chilean Winter', a protest organised by high school and college students, who demanded changes in the free-market policy governing education, energy and the environment (Valenzuela et al. 2012). This interaction between media and civic engagment has also been studied in societies within the region that do not have a strong mobilisation tradition (Welp and Wheatley 2012). The anti-corruption movement and the spontaneous mobilisation among middle class and young people against transportation costs and corruption in Brazil in July 2013 are likewise examples of social media being used extensively as a means of disseminating protest (Moseley and Layton 2013). It is worth noticing that Argentina, Uruguay, Chile and Brazil are among the Latin American countries with the greatest Internet usage. However, connectivity is not the sole determining factor shaping social media and protest in Latin America. An historical tradition of mobilisation and the experience protest may play a role where connectivity is low. The mobilisation against the construction of a cement plant at the border of the national park Los Haitises in the Dominican Republic is a case in point. In countries with low Internet access and weak mobilisation tradition, activists have made extensive use of social media in their protests, and have achieved significant results according to Welp and Wheatley (2012). The protest against pulp mills and forest monoculture in Uruguay and Argentina mainly involved middle class, middle-aged activists, some of them well experienced in traditional mobilisation strategies. This chapter sets out to investigate the role played by digital media as a means to disseminate information on environmental concerns publicly, and organise mobilisation in a region where the mere formulation of environmental concerns is problematic. In such a context, environmental mobilisation becomes a sort of balancing act between trying to capture media attention through spectacular physical mobilisations and negotiating public opinion around environmental themes. This case is not representative of all environmental movements in Latin America but it offers theoretical insights into the interplay between digital media and environmental protest in non-Western socio-economic and cultural settings.

Background

The last thirty years' succession of democratically elected governments, with almost no interruptions through *coups d'état*, have provided the necessary political framework for strengthening civil society organisations and their initiatives in Latin America. Environmental movements, in particular, experienced a resurgence in the 1990s. These movements focused on finding solutions to specific problems, at a national or regional level, in coordination with governments, universities and research centres, and have therefore seen their legitimacy increased (Calderón 2012, 233). However, environmental concerns are often left off of the political agenda and ignored in mainstream media. Data from the International Telecommunication Union (ITU) and Internet World Stats (IWS) places Argentina, Uruguay, Brazil and Chile among the most intensive users of the Internet in the region of the Southern Cone, in particular Argentina, Uruguay and Chile. General connectivity rates increased rapidly in the 2000s. Over 50% of the population in these countries had access to the Internet in 2010, compared to 30% in 2005 (Calderón 2012). About 100% of all Argentineans and Uruguayans had a mobile phone in 2008 (Bibolini and Baker 2009, 252).

One of the most significant environmental conflicts in recent years in Latin America, both in terms of the number of people involved, national, regional and international political repercussions, and the duration of mainstream media coverage, took place in connection with the establishment of two pulp mills by the Finnish-owned Metsä-Botnia (hereafter Botnia) and the Spanish-owned Empresa Nacional de Celulosa España (Ence). These pulp mills were to be established on the Uruguayan side of the Uruguay River, the geographical and political border between Argentina and Uruguay. The protest movement initially had three main driving groups: the Asamblea Ciudadana Ambiental de Gualeguayú (ACAG) — a grassroots organisation with its base in Argentina — and the environmental NGOs Grupo Guayubira and REDES Amigos de la Tierra, based in Uruguay. From 2005 to 2008, these organisations led the fight against the construction of pulp mills, at first in unison and later separately. The Uruguayan NGOs also protested against the cultivation of eucalyptus trees in Uruguay. This non-native, fast-growing tree provides raw material for the pulp industry.

The movement began to take shape in 2005, when 40,000 people from Argentina and Uruguay gathered to block the traffic on a bridge linking the two countries. The blockades and protests continued tenaciously until 2009 and one of the bridges was blockaded for two years, closed for both cargo and private traffic. The protest actions and the authorities' difficulties in reaching an agreement on the location and control of the planned pulp mills severely disrupted diplomatic relations between Argentina and Uruguay. The diplomatic conflict was initially dealt with through bilateral negotiations, but when these failed, the countries' governments sought international assistance to solve their differences. They entreated the Spanish king, Juan Carlos de Borbón to mediate between them, and appealed to the Regional Court of Justice of the Southern Common Market, Mercosur (formed at this point in time by a regional agreement between Argentina, Brazil, Paraguay and Uruguay), as well as to the International Court of Justice in The Hague. The International Court of Justice reached a verdict in 2010, which brought an end to the activists' blockade. This eased the diplomatic tensions, though it did not completely silence dissent.

As a consequence of the intense protest actions, the Spanish plant was, in fact, never built. The Finnish plant was eventually built, but is now subject to stricter environmental monitoring than had been stipulated before the protests took place. The plant is now being monitored both formally, by the nations involved, and informally, by citizen groups. Today, the groups are still active, but no longer work in unison. Their main vehicles for dissent through online platforms, e.g. websites, Facebook, YouTube, and Twitter, rather than protests.

Digital Media and Protest

The field of media studies has set out to understand the rapid changes in the organisation of dissent that have come with the widespread availability of digital media. Of particular concern are those civil society actors who rely heavily on digital media when embarking on protest actions (Rodríguez et al. 2014). Many scholars have highlighted the synergies between the Internet and the non-hierarchical, flexible, identity-based, decentralised, autonomous and loosely structured networks of social movements (MacCaughey and Ayers 2003; van de Donk et al. 2004; de Jong et al. 2005; Leivrouw 2011). In addition, it has been stressed that the use of digital information technologies considerably increases activists' chances of disseminating alternative discourses, as these groups might find it difficult or impossible to enter the public sphere through mainstream media (Coyer et al. 2007; Bailey et al. 2008; Atkinson 2010). Some argue that social media have provided new prospects for organising and have accelerated the dissemination of contentious politics among citizens and civil society organisations to a degree hitherto unimagined (Shirky 2011). Such capability has probably enhanced the activists' chances of reaching the mainstream media globally (Cottle 2011). This has bearing on the dissemination of protests beyond regional and national territories.

At the same time, it has been argued that the logic of protest action itself is changing, which makes it necessary to look into the organisation of dissent in different ways. Analysing protests organised recently Lance Bennett and Alexandra Segerberg (2011) advance the concept of 'connective action' as a way to distinguish the mobilisations basically driven from social media from 'collective action', where the role of established ations is more prominent. However, beyond the discussion on the distinction between collective and connective action, when it comes to the organisation of protest to achieve predefined goals, a pure instrumental role of media seems to be generally rejected as a standpoint (Carrol and Hackett 2006; Downing 2008; Treré 2012). This is because collective action is considered communicative *per se*, since social movements occupy a space defined by the participants' mode of interaction and mode of engagement. In this 'collective action space' multiple communication strategies and technologies can be adapted as the situation demands (Bimber, Flanagin and Stohl 2012). It is then necessary to study the whole range of media practices, the relationships among them and the political, economic and cultural context in which they are embedded, in order to comprehend how media practices form part of the processes of organising protest actions.

On the other hand, less optimistic observers signal that the use of the Internet for communication among activists makes them easily traceable by governments that wish to hunt down and punish either individual activists or networks of people and organisations (Morozov 2011; Leistert 2013). This obviously influences the use of these digital technologies for the organisation of dissent and, in practice, reduces their potential impact on democratisation processes. Empirically, there is evidence that well-established, environmental NGOs make relatively little use of the Internet, even in the media-saturated contexts of some Western societies (Kenix 2007; Stein 2009; Waters et al. 2009). As these groups display low levels of information, mobilisation, interactivity both on their websites and social network pages, it may indicate that their organisational structures do not always make use of the Internet's opportunities to the degree postulated and celebrated in some literature (Stein 2009) This is mainly the case for more or less established organisations in industrialised countries. More empirical research in media systems, like the Latin American one, is still necessary but some evidence suggests a similar trend (Melián 2012).

In this respect, the notion of 'media practice', as discussed by Nick Couldry (2004) is useful. This is the idea that the principles of media-oriented practices are generated in the social world. These are to be found in people's understanding, not in researchers' *a priori* conceptualisations. Because media also represent the social world, they inevitably mediate such practices. Thus media practices have direct consequences on how social norms are defined and ordered. This is not to say that all practices are mediated but that significant social practices are represented and sometimes organised through media. To put emphasis on media practices means to focus on the understanding of the principles whereby, and the mechanisms through which, these practices are ordered. Media practice theory helps scholars approach the kinds of tasks people are perform with media as well as what people say about media. For activists, actions are then weaved into a practice not just by explicit understandings, but also by the governance of shared rules and references, such as projects and beliefs. In this way, the conditions and limitations of activists' media practices correspond to a shared framework that shows a deep sense of interconnectedness with the particular socio-cultural and political context studied. The aim here is to explore the ways activists within the movement in question used new digital media tools and formulated an environmental narrative against the backdrop of the particular mobilisation traditions and historical context of Latin America.

The Study

The study of social movements is generally complex, because these are fluid and flexible social configurations that are difficult to assess even in terms of duration (Melucci 1996). The study of digital media practices also poses difficulties because they are not easy to observe. Many studies of the media practices of social movements focus on one type of media, most often the movements' websites such as in the work of Laura Stein (2011). Other scholars have focused on the movements' posts on social media platforms such as Facebook or Twitter as in the work of Bennet and Segerberg (2011). In a departure from this methodology we rely here on semi-structured interviews with all the activists in charge of communication tasks in the three main groups of the movement (9 in total), the groups' homepages from 2005 to 2008 (a total of 190), and selected texts on these websites published during the same period (a total of 24). As far as the selection of activists interviewed is concerned, I focus entirely on those who were in charge of communication tasks. A representative sample of activists from each group would not have been ideal, as I am concerned with the communication practices of the groups involved in the movement rather than on such practices at the individual level. Because the interviews target those in charge of communication tasks, the perspective of many other activists involved in the groups are left out of the study. One reason for choosing this method is the difficulty of, in the case of the ACAG, identifying and interviewing activists within a loose network of individuals, and in the case of the NGOs, of interviewing people who did not actually work with communication tasks. Another factor is that the activists directly involved in communication tasks within the groups had greater influence within the movement when it came to determining and executing these tasks. This probably also gave these activists a wider perspective of the numerous aspects involved in the organisation and execution of these tasks.

David Silverman (2006) calls this approach 'purposive sampling' as the empirical material used aims at illuminating the specific media practices on which I focus. The use of interviews offers advantages because informants described practices that occurred in the recent past from their own perspectives. At the same time, this approach has limitations in the sense that informants provide the interviewer with a reconstruction of the practices. However, interviews were preferable to dependence on empirical material generated by participant observation, which would not have been possible in a study such as this one. I analyse the websites because they were the preferred online platform within this movement, and by homing in on some selected texts I perform the kind of deeper discourse analysis that better illuminates the importance of these websites to the movement.

Thematic analysis was the method selected to analyse the interviews as it enabled the organisation of material according to the themes informants dealt with while maintaining the theoretical framework of the study. This analytical strategy implies a 'pattern matching' technique where similar or alternative patterns regarding the theoretical points of departure are sought and analysed in the empirical materials with the goal of building an explanatory approach (Yin 2003).

To analyse the websites I adapted Malin Sveningsson, Mia Lövheim, and Magnus Bergquist's (2003) model because it was suitable for mapping the structure of websites in accordance with their main functions. Furthermore, my discussion of selected texts from these web pages has been informed by Norman Fairclough's (1995) model for discourse analysis, because this method facilitates the analysis of power relations as represented in the texts, which reflect the power relations in which the activists were immersed.

Camouflaged Arguments

In societies where environmental concerns rank low, activists make an effort to present their arguments in terms that may appeal to both the populace and mainstream media. One way of doing this, as shown by the analysis, is to transfer discursive tropes from themes that enjoy high status to themes that are considered less relevant. It is a way of packaging environmental concerns within more easily recognizable discursive frames, often those commonly used by mainstream news media. In this manner, a low-status subject matter can be associated with an issue that is considered very relevant in a particular socio-cultural context. It is a way of increasing the apparent importance of the matter dealt with. The process of representing a certain issue as associated with another frame of discourse is a process of transformation, which involves what might be termed discourse camouflage.

The organisation websites studied here functioned as platforms from which activists had the opportunity to formulate their concerns and claims. In Uruguay, in particular, websites were the sole platform where activists could voice their concerns, as mainstream media did not regularly make use of them as sources of information. The Argentinean mainstream media, on the other hand, used Argentinean and even Uruguayan activists as sources, mainly on the issue of the physical protests. The groups' websites remain, then, the most important arena for activists to express arguments in their own terms.

The analysis of these websites shows that the activists' claims were not directly formulated in environmental terms but were, in fact, framed in terms of political and economic consequences, especially where these clains concerned the social impact of the pulp mills and of forest monoculture. These political and economic arguments were sometimes linked to concerns about health problems, but without further specification of what would be the tangible consequences for human health. Arguments relating specifically to the consequences of pulp mills and forest monoculture for soil, water, air, flora, and fauna were rarely used. The environmental impact of pulp mills and forest monoculture was not presented as a forceful argument. Furthermore, the very word 'environment' was often absent from the activists' argumentation. The following are examples of how the activists' discourse was instead informed by political and economic concerns:

> [The blockade] will help to establish a common oppositional front to the negative effects that will be registered in tourism, sports fishing, apiculture and agriculture on both sides of the Uruguay River. (Published by REDES on 29 April, 2005)

> It becomes evident for the world that the national policy of the state is determined by a multinational and that the government of Mr Tabaré Vázquez is on its knees before the interest of Botnia, giving away the sovereignty of Uruguayans. (Published by ACAG on 9 November, 2007)

> Until when will our government officials continue exchanging our rich patrimony for small mirrors and colourful beads? (Published by Guayubira Group on 30 April, 2005)

The activists connected politics and protest on various levels. Firstly, the protest was linked discursively to contemporary national politics, and the relationship of this politics to global capital. This was the case, for instance, when it was repeatedly argued that support for the development of pulp mills and the forestry industry in the country was inconsistent with the political model that the ruling party defended before coming into power. The left coalition had traditionally opposed granting foreign capital benefits at the expense of natural resources. Approval for the construction of pulp mills, and thus the expansion of the forest model in practice, was seen as a hard retreat on the promised political positioning.

The discursive interconnection between the protest and political argumentations became evident at another level: historical references linked the present situation to the colonial past. A parallel was established between the colonial past and the current political situation, described as post-colonial. Comparisons were made between the welcoming attitude of native people towards the Spanish and contemporary governments' willingness to allow transnational companies to operate in these countries. The protest was conceived through a frame of post-colonial relationships between local and regional governance and the economic power of global companies. Activists depicted the post-colonial condition as the reluctance of contemporary Latin-American governments, in this case, Uruguay, to remain in control of national policies and regulations. Accusations were made that the governments sacrificed national resources, such as land and water, in the name of globalisation and for the benefit of national finances.

Evidently, the argumentation from historical analogies and references to contemporary political activities implied a local or regional Spanish-speaking audience well versed both in the region's current affairs and is history. This indicates that it was never the intention of these activists to reach a more global audience. However, even though the various groups had similar lines of argumentation, and appealed to the same kind of reader, the ways in which their arguments were introduced and displayed on their websites varied greatly. While the Argentinean grassroots group mainly used slogans, short texts and visual elements, such as illustrations or pictures, to make their claims, the Uruguayan NGOs provided a wealth of texts of a reflective nature. This establishes a distinction between the ways in which different kinds of organisations arranged their online content. The use of slogans and short texts has been associated with loose formations that could be linked to the logic of connective action, while the use of long explanatory texts is more typical of established organisations within social movements. This case acted as confirmation. The grassroots organisation, which organised spontaneously in order to protest, preferred to communicate its discontent through the use of slogans and short texts. The environmental NGOs, active long before this protest and concerned with other contemporary issues, preferred to use longer and more in-depth texts to formulate their critique.

User-Generated Content and Mainstream Media

Websites were conceived as public space belonging to activists. They were the online representation of the activists' goals and *raison d'être* during all the years the conflict lasted. This online record was also seen as a way of positioning the organisation among other actors within the public sphere. In the process of appropriating this space, activists made choices about whether or not to formulate their opinions and concerns, as this implied a public positioning that could be harmful for them. The relationship between the protest groups and the respective national mainstream media greatly shaped how the informants conceptualised the online content they created. Activists working for the NGOs felt the Uruguayan mainstream media had aligned their discourse with the government's closing all doors to reach the public in this way. Thus, the online content produced by the Uruguayan NGOs was considered the only way to reach citizens with counteractive information. It provided space for alternative perspectives, which were perceived as otherwise excluded from journalistic coverage. The online content was viewed as 'balanced' because it included alternative sources that were never utilised by mainstream media. Informants did not argue that they represented an objective stance but that they contributed to objectivity by disclosing themes, arguments and voices otherwise excluded. They saw their online media presence, therefore, as a sort of balancing act, or at least intended it as such. Websites became the only venues for expressing dissent when the NGOs ceased supporting blockades as the main form of protest (blockades were only continued by the Argentinean grassroots group). Even though NGOs ceased supporting the blockades, these activists were not used as sources by mainstream media.

Constraints on the formulation of content related to contextual political issues did, however, blunt the counteractive character of the Uruguayan activists' online output. The fact that Uruguay was ruled by a left-wing coalition greatly affected how they chose to express themselves. In practice, it determined the type of information that would be published on their websites, as well as the tone in which it was presented. Traditionally supportive of the ruling left coalition, the Uruguayan activists certainly used their websites to formulate public critiques, but they weighed their words carefully. In the beginning of the period under study, open criticism of the government was considered as nearly tantamount to political treason among these activists. Activists, aware of the nationalistic tone that had become associated with the issue of the construction of pulp mills in Uruguay, even in the mainstream media, were afraid of positioning themselves too clearly at the risk of becoming isolated on other issues. Later, when contesting views were practically banned from the mainstream news media, partly due to pressure exerted by the state, whose advertising was important to the economic survival of the media, the websites' content became more radical, more openly oppositional to government policies.

ACAG informants, on the other hand, did not see their online publishing as the only way to reach out to the citizens. They felt they could easily contact both local and national mainstream media, at least on the issue of the actual blockades. Instead, Argentinean activists used the organisation's website, e-mails and newsletters to present themselves, their protest actions and resolutions, or short pieces of information about future events or past incidents. They felt that by using their website in this manner, they controlled a 'public space' from which they could publish information they considered relevant at exactly the time they wished. As mentioned above, there were no attempts to formulate long and explicative counteractive accounts. Activists explained this in terms of the potential audience they could reach. They preferred to talk directly to journalists because they considered mainstream news media a far more effective means of reaching a large number of people. These activists were frequently journalistic sources on the issue of the physical mobilisations. However, they did not engage in explicative argumentations about the environmental consequences of the pulp and forest industries at any length, either with the journalists or on their website.

Networking beyond the Digital

Informants agreed that the Internet was used extensively as a means for engagement, for establishing a network that linked the different groups, other organisations and citizens in the region and beyond. Informants assessed the digital exchange as unique, firstly because it provided valuable insights, arguments and information, which were not to be found elsewhere, especially not in the mainstream media. Secondly, it was considered of key importance because it was the only possible way of divulging information generated by the groups of activists. This positioning coincides with the notion of 'social movement media' that include counter-information produced by voices often excluded from mainstream media (Downing 2008).

The use of the Internet for disseminating information, and for collecting insights about the forest industry from around the world, increased significantly during the studied period. For example, in 2005 the ACAG operated with a list of fifty e-mail addresses; by 2007 the number of addressees had had grown to two thousand, counting individuals, mainstream media and other environmental organisations or 'asambleas', 250 of these being activists from Gualeguaychú. Guayubira also increased the number of people listed during the period studied, and by 2009 they had 1000 contacts that they regularly kept informed about the state of the protest. In addition, lists of e-mail accounts of members of parliament and of mainstream media journalists were used for sending specific information about activist claims and activities.

Networking was rarely used for promoting participation on online campaigns. A small number of online campaigns, listed on one of the websites, show that this possibility was used only to a limited extent. Informants said that online campaigns were not considered the primary method of protest. Instead, e-mails and newsletters served as the means of disseminating information to generate awareness and offline engagement (from participation in meetings, workshops, conferences to attendance to the physical mobilisations). This is because of their multiplication effect in weaving online and offline networks. Often the exchange of information was initiated digitally, but was expanded through the generation of instances of information exchange that compensated for the existent digital divide. In praxis, the content of e-mails and newsletters sent by activists was printed out and discussed at meetings and workshops held among people with very limited access to e-mail. Local radio broadcasts informing people about the protest and the arguments behind it were also based on this material. This combination of digital and analogue media practices illustrates how a digital divide, still present in the region, was overcome to some degree.

Networking with organisations and individuals situated outside of the region was less frequent than networking within the region. When contacts were made with organisations or people outside of the region, it was for the purpose of exchanging information about the forest industry and about campaigns against pulp mills in other parts of the world. The environmental NGOs, which already had contact with global environmental organisations concerned with forest exploitation and/or pulp mills, made frequent use of these links. However, they did not seek their support to initiate digital mobilisations that could propagate beyond the region. Physical actions, which implied the participation of the local populace and regional organisations, were the preferred means of mobilisation. A strong mobilisation tradition, both in Argentina and Uruguay, may explain why these activists relied on proven ways of protesting, such as the blockade.

On the other hand, all the groups found global networking vital for meeting the enormous demand for information on pulp mill technology, forest industry development and environmental activism, information which was not to be found locally, particularly during the first years of the protest. The NGO informants had worked with the issue of monoculture of eucalyptus trees before, but they had hardly any knowledge of pulp mills. ACAG informants began reading about pulp mills and the forest industry when the movement first started. 'We had a permanent exchange of information, advice and coordination locally and globally. Globally we were in contact with the WRM (World Rainforest Movement) and organisations in Spain regarding Ence, Finland regarding Botnia and in general with Portugal, and then regionally with Brazil, Argentina and Chile' (Male, REDES). This contact was purely geared towards getting information about the industry. Also, web searches in general were judged to be of great importance when it came to understanding the consequences of pulp mills and forest monoculture. Some of the interviewees referred to web searches as magical and even nurturing. These searches, together with the information exchange with organisations in other regions, improved the activists' understanding of forest industry and pulp mills, and helped them formulate their arguments. An example of how global discourses, via the Internet, influenced the movement's formulations is a key slogan used by the ACAG, which reads, 'Gualeguaychú does not give social license to Botnia'. One of the informants from the ACAG, during his Internet searches, became very interested in the notion of 'social license', which had been used in Canada. The term refers to how companies should strive to gain the support of the community that will be affected by their activities before actually initiating any changes. Fascinated with the idea, he spread the understanding of this notion within the ACAG. Soon after, the term was widely applied by the ACAG activists. In the years to come this slogan would be used on their websites, banners, stickers, and t-shirts.

Mobile Personal Engagement

Although activists had access to mobile phones during the whole period, it was not viewed as being crucial to the organisation of collective action among these informants. Mobile communication practices *per se* were not seen as something that could spark civic engagement. Informants assigned less importance to mobile phones than the Internet when it came to mobilisation and communication of collective action, and they did not consider mobile phones a fundamental medium of communication or intervention for grassroots movements and political activism as shown, for instance, by Manuel Castells (2009). Rather, they considered the mobile phone a means of person-to-person communication. Its private character, as perceived by informants, had to do with the range of imagined possibilities mobile communication granted for civic engagement in this context. Certainly, technology *per se* does not initiate dissent. The actualisation of the possibilities enabled by technologies within particular contexts, which create particular collective action spaces that host civic activities, is marked both by convention and innovation and depends on the surrounding conditions and the imagined (or unimagined) possibilities that attend them (Papacharissi 2010).

However, even though the mobile phones practices were associated with the private sphere, it became clear, as a result of the interviews, that in practice they had an important role in mobilisation. The ACAG activists used mobile phones when organising actual physical demonstrations, as these required detailed organisation before, during and after the event. Some activists had a system for distributing urgent messages by using mobile phones. Chains of text messages were agreed on for cases of emergency. When an activist had something urgent to communicate, he or she would send a text message to the activist who was next on a ready-made list, who would then send pass it on, and so on, until the circle was completed. This system assured that the message would be sent to all the people involved at a minimum cost for each individual. Text messages were primarily distributed through established personal networks. This is consistent with the findings of current research on the personal character of mobile phone communication (Villi 2011).

Accessibility was another defining feature of the activists' mobile phone practices. The fact that the mobile phone was available regardless of time or place made it an important means of communicating among themselves and with journalists. Whether people were located in different cities and areas, or were performing blockades in the middle of the countryside, mobile phones were used to maintain active contact amongst the informants whenever needed. Mobile phones were used as windows onto the blockade actions, as a way of taking part from a distance. This possibility allowed informants to 'be there' even though the protests occurred in different locations, sometimes simultaneously, and often far apart. In this sense, activists were able to deploy spectacular physical demonstrations in isolated places, far from these countries' capitals, while still staying in contact with each other and being aware of each other's actions.

The accessibility provided by mobile phones was also utilised during extraordinary events. In such cases, mobile phones were used in order to rapidly distribute information through the personal networks of activists. These channels could then disseminate the information further, among the media as well. Mobile phones were able to accelerate the generation and dissemination of content (text and images) when extraordinary events associated with protest actions took place. However, at this time, mobile phone cameras were mainly put into use when these extraordinary circumstances had to be documented visually. It is important to remember that the use of pictures is linked to the technology. Mobile phones were not, at this time, smartphones. Accordingly, activists were not able to use the Internet as a cheap means for distributing pictures. They used the telephone line for sending images. The cost of sending these images (considerably more expensive than sending texts) limited the use of mobile phones among the informants, and gave pictures a special status. Something 'important' had to happen if a picture was to be distributed. The production of documentation for activists' claims was considered such an occasion. Clearly this has changed with the introduction and popularisation of smartphones with Internet connections, which has created an enormous flow of images taken with mobile phones on social media. Pictures of a big stain in the river's water were sent, for instance, to support activists' claims of contamination of the river. Initially distributed by mobile phones to journalists and activists in charge of communications, these images were rapidly published on the websites and further distributed via e-mail, the cheapest option at this time. Images published on websites or distributed by e-mail often had contextualising captions to reinforce the message that the activists wanted to convey. Images captured by mobile phones were conceived as unique value generators, which added a sense of affirmation and importance.

The ability to stay in contact through mobile phones contributed to their sense of togetherness even when they were far apart. Mobile phones contributed, then, to a sense of belonging and comradeship among some of the informants. Informants saw receiving and sending text messages as important measures that helped them deal emotionally with drawbacks and failures. They could express feelings, provide support and receive encouragement. The act of writing and sending a text that would remain on someone else's screen, or receiving a text that could be read several times afterwards, was viewed as a concrete way of providing and receiving the encouragement necessary for further engagement.

> When a comrade was lying in hospital severely injured (during a protest) I received a text message with every step that was being taken by the doctors. I wrote back and asked them to come closer to him and tell him that I was there. (Woman, ACAG)

Another feature of the use of mobile phone was coupled to issues of personal safety. Maintaining a blockade of an international bridge in solitary places was not always a smooth process. People became angry, especially when the blockades were not permanent — causing delays in crossing the bridge and sometimes forcing people to wait hours before the activists would let them through. The mobile phone often provided a sense of personal safety. Informants participating in the blockades felt they were not 'alone' if they had their mobiles at hand. They felt they were always able to contact the police or other activists or the media from the middle of the countryside. The use of mobile phones meant, again, being in contact at a distance. It was a means of obtaining help in the case of an emergency. Under the circumstances, the help could not arrive immediately, but the mobile phone represented a sort of connection to somewhere else and someone else besides those involved in the actual situation. The connection was as real for the person calling as for the person listening to the conversation, or witnessing the message being sent or received.

Opportunities for Public Debate

Digital media offers increased opportunities for public debate on various online platforms. Whether people debate within like-minded groups or engage in discussions with those who represent other beliefs, public debate must be considered relevant for the promotion of awareness, which again may prompt or strengthen civic engagement. Accordingly, debate generally plays a positive role for democracy and for society (Dahlgren 2007). At this time and amongst these informants, online public debate was in fact not viewed as an opportunity to promote awareness and, in turn, the civic engagement of citizens. The informants did not recognise their websites, existing blogs or other online platforms as opportunities to promote a 'serious' debate on the issue. Rather they argued that ongoing discussions on these forums were focused mainly on the blockade as a means of protest, not on the benefits and disadvantages of the installation of pulp mills in Uruguay or the development of the forest industry in the country, which expanded forest monoculture in order to provide raw material for these plants. Nor did these informants perceive the discussions as a way of provoking a wide debate on the consequences of the construction of the pulp mills. Neither blogs nor online forums were viewed as places where one could engage in constructive public debate. Generally, online debates were perceived as serving the interests of the pulp mill companies and/or personal interests (people trying to gain points from governmental officials or the companies). They did not think the online discussions contributed to a meaningful exchange of opinions and arguments; rather, they saw these spaces in which some explicitly nationalistic points of views were formulated. The informants were aware of the existence of a blogosphere around the movement against the pulp mills but they did not actively engage in it. Some of the informants had made comments on these platforms on rare occasions, but had not engaged actively in these debates, nor with supporters or opponents. The existing online debate opportunities were seen as venues for radicalised and personal opinions, either defending or rejecting the blockade of the river in nationalistic terms.

The analysis of the NGOs' websites shows that they were not actively used to promote public debate on the issue. Discussion forums were basically unavailable. Guayubira and REDES activists explicitly rejected and rarely even discussed having interactive features, according to the informants. They conceived their websites mainly as places to make their beliefs and arguments available to those who wanted to read them, but did not go so far as to initiate an online dialogue. Alternative interactive ways of promoting the participation of citizens were only available on the website of the grassroots group. Grassroots activists were more interested in opening up possibilities for public participation, but they did not explicitly conceive their websites as places to facilitate online dialogue, since participation was regulated. Still, the website of the grassroots organisation provided readers with some opportunity to share user-generated content in the form of pictures, videos and texts by submitting them to the Webmaster (far from full-fledged interactivity).

As on other issues, the grassroots movement and the NGOs differed in their conception of online public debate. NGO activists had an unspoken understanding that they were not to use blogs as a place for debate. They did not participate as individuals and only made comments, in cases when they felt compelled to answer a direct attack. ACAG members agreed that blogs were a hostile arena for debating the protest, but most of them had published comments on an individual basis from time to time — sometimes anonymously. The activists viewed anonymous participation positively, because it allowed them to abandon discussions in which the tone became too aggressive. When they gave their names, they felt compelled to continue participating in the discussion. Anonymity did not, however, promote meaningful debate. Informants reacted against what they perceived as outright aggressive comments, often expressed in nationalistic terms. Papacharissi has argued that certain forms of heated online exchange can be understood as expressions of keen interest and even as a necessary element when face-to-face communication does not exist (Papacharissi 2004). However, informants generally avoided heated exchanges, suggesting that fierce online arguments could be avoided if they sought out online platforms that reflected their own opinions.

Although awareness of various kinds of online public debates did not translate into active participation among informants, there were those who, at the time of the interviews (September 2009), had begun to question this inactivity, or at least to reflect on it. Some of the

Uruguayan activists considered the need to start looking at social media such as Facebook and Twitter as means of disseminating the campaign, as these social networks were then becoming more popular. Some ACAG informants were not content with the limited interactivity on the website. They complained about missed opportunities for spreading protest action via social media. Some did not think it sufficed to publish comments, pictures, videos, illustrations, music, and documents sent by people via the website's e-mail. They explained that this had not been possible due to, on the one hand, a lack of resources and, on the other, the particular character of the protest movement, as the movement defined itself through demonstrations, not online protests. Again, the fact that social media were becoming popular at this time, and that these activists were middle-aged, may explain their attitude to the use of various kinds of interactive, online platforms.

Civic Engagement and Media Practice

Activists' Internet and mobile phone practices reflected how an understanding of the relationship between civic engagement and digital media depends upon factors such as type of organisation, age of activists involved, and their previous experience with more traditional forms of mobilisation, beyond access to digital technology. Although the activists interviewed had access to the Internet from the beginning of the period studied, and used it to formulate and disseminate their arguments in order to seek offline engagement, access new information and contact environmental organisations in other parts of the world, patterns of Internet-based media practices and understanding were nevertheless linked to factors such as type of organisation, age and the previous mobilisation experience.

Depending on the type of organisations activists viewed digital media use differently, either purely organisational versus personal in the case of NGOs activists, or as personal practice driven by the protest's interest in the case of the grassroots activists. NGO activists viewed media practices as something belonging exclusively to the activities performed via the organisation. They made a clear distinction between their organisational and their personal digital media practices. NGO activists used the organisations' channels to act in the name of the organisation. Personal digital media practices were not considered suitable for promoting the organisation's activities or arguments. They separated them in this way:

> The colleagues that worked more with the campaign had the task of representing REDES. This is an internal organisation issue. Even though I belong to REDES I cannot give personal opinions. (Man, REDES)

On the other hand, grassroots activists conceived media digital practices as something integral to both their participation in the ACAG and to their personal initiatives in relation to the movement. For instance, they all produced, post and re-post information on the movement, the protests and also on other environmental and social protests or organisations in the region. In addition, grassroots activists perceived digital media practices as something empowering, because it gave them the opportunity to contact individuals and organisations directly. Able to get in contact with journalists, experts and organisations grassroots activists felt they could make people or organisations accountable in regards to what they did or said on the media. Opportunities created by digital media gave them a sense of personal empowerment by giving them the chance to quiz experts, to make political officials and companies accountable for their decisions or arguments.

> To those of us who are aware and have the time to devote to it, the Internet gives us the opportunity to act upon something. Not everybody does it but you can communicate directly with those who launch the news and demand that they prove what they are saying and if you do it by e-mail you know it's written. (Man, ACAG)

The quality and political economy of Internet access also deem important, and even defining, for activists' digital media practices. Access to the Internet either at work or at home and the speed of the connection were influential factors shaping the media practices of activists. The speed and cost of connections, not only among informants but also among people in general, shaped activists' digital media practices. Text was preferable to images or videos. The use of images and videos was less significant and sporadic. Images and videos take more time to download and/or send than text, an important fact considering the varied quality and the high cost of the connections available. While the NGOs' members had access to fast Internet connections at the office, members of the grassroots organisation had Internet access, of varying speed quality, and only at home. Often grassroots activists shared the connection with several neighbours in an informal arrangement that granted lower costs at the expense of speed. Only one of them had access to the organisation's old computer installed in the organisation's office, a room lent by the House of Culture in Gualeguaychú, part of the city's municipality. The organisation's e-mail account was organised via g-mail, from which, at that time, a maximum of 2000 e-mails could be sent per day. Slow connections and limited e-mail traffic played a role when one planned online mobilisations or the dissemination of information in general. When it came to mobilisation, other forms of communication (posters, car stickers, and face-to-face encounters) were also used to invite people to participate in the protest actions.

The type of organisation, either an established NGO or a grassroots movement, influenced the structure, content and strategy of their of activists' digital media practices. Communication roles were performed and organised in different ways. NGOs had established criteria and greater resources (people, time, money) for the communication activities, including the digital output. The grassroots organisation relied mainly on voluntary work, and on individual decisions rather than on centrally structured group criteria when it comes to their communication activities. Each of the groups had one or two people in charge of communication: a full-time worker in the case of REDES and ACAG (their only paid position) and a part-time worker at Guayubira. While the NGO activists considered communication with the outside a collaborative effort, which should be communicated via the spokesperson of the organisation, the 'asamblea' had a more flexible view. Grassroots activists could, via the Internet or by mobile phone, communicate individually with mainstream media and other connected individuals. Their communications did not have to be coordinated with the rest of the organisation.

Another important factor was the age of the interviewed activists, which played a role in the kind of media practices that were perceived as appropriate and valuable for civic engagement activities. In a discussion of the new social movement for curbing climate change, for example, Castells notes: 'Besides Indymedia, numerous hack labs, temporary or stable, populated the movement and used the superior technological savvy of the new generation to build and advantage in the communication battle against their elders in the mainstream media'

(Castells 2009, 344). In a more empirically based discussion of activists as interpretive communities, Rauch interviewed snowball-selected activists. She found that for the most part they were in their late teens and early twenties (Rauch 2007).

The average age of the activists involved in communication tasks in this movement was 41, with the youngest being 25 and the oldest being 57. Moreover, in terms of age, they were quite representative of their respective organisations. In my fieldwork, I observed that people working in the NGOs and those involved in the organisation of the ACAG's protest activities were around 40 years of age. Furthermore, the informants confirmed these observations during the interviews. Interestingly, the exception was the many young people who participated in the actual protests organised by the 'asamblea'. In effect, informants confirmed that young people showed their engagement by participating in the mobilisations organised by the older activists. However, these young people were absent from the actual organisation of the protests, discussions and weekly meetings. Informants believed this to have had an effect on the ways in which the Internet was used by the ACAG.

> I realise that this technological battle (referring to young people's use of Facebook and Twitter), this technological tool, was misused by us. Maybe there is time still. We have had a 'young assembly' but we haven't been able to use it in this sense. It's an immense and terrific tool. (Man, ACAG)

On the other hand, Guayubira and REDES informants defined their Internet and mobile phone practices in opposition to young people's use of social media and in terms of civic participation styles. But contrary to ACAG informants, they did not perceive social media as an opportunity for furthering participation and agency among people. They considered Facebook a mere tool for distributing personal content and entertainment, and therefore underestimated the possibility of using Facebook for civic engagement. Traditional mobilisation patterns were still the norm, and the Uruguayan NGOs, more established and well trained in the arts of mobilisation in the countryside, simply did not see social media as an opportunity. They did not expect to reach the stakeholders they wished to influence, such as politicians and journalists, through social media, because at the time these were mainly perceived as a personal communicational arena used by young people, uninterested in environmental concerns or in politics in general.

> From what I see of Facebook it is basically a way to transfer of personal information to public spaces. This has nothing to do with our activity, and it has nothing to do with anything substantial. It is a lot of people, knowing about other people, to what party they went, what they wore then, how much alcohol they drank, how many pictures they took, one million pictures. This is far from what Guayubira is. (Woman, Guayubira Group)

Digital media grew in importance among activists during the years to come. Even though they had different perspectives, informants shared an instrumentalist conception of digital media practices, which they considered suitable primarily for one-way communication. They associated websites, newsletters, and e-mails with a form of information transfer taking place between them and others under more controlled and 'serious' forms. Social media was associated with young people and not related as much to traditional forms of civic engagement or modes of protest. It is worth noting that social media were becoming popular in 2008. However, this is insufficient to explain informants' assessment. Rather, it illustrates how they understood their digital media practices in terms of different styles of civic engagement. Interviews with members of the grassroots organisation suggest that the relationship between civic engagement and digital media was in the process of becoming a more 'social' form of networking, while NGO members had a more traditional one-way view on their digital media practices.

Conclusion

The relation between environmental movements and digital media in non-Western media systems, such as the Southern Cone, changes with the emergence of new informational circumstances that give citizens and civil society organisations greater access to digital media that enables them to reach fellow citizens often, while bypassing mainstream media. During this long-standing protest, a combination of digital media practices enabled the formulation of arguments on the activists' terms and the exchange and dissemination of these among activists and other citizens and environmental organisations, both locally and globally. Although its organisation and dissemination were aided by the use of online platforms and networking, physical mobilisation was central to the protest. Despite the fact that these countries have the highest Internet use in Latin America, activists relied primerely on a well-tested and widely used form of mobilisation in the region: the blockade. This may be due to the fact that the majority of activists were middle-aged, and that some of them were well trained in traditional forms of activism.

Overall, this case helps raise some theoretical points about digital media and protest in non-Western contexts. Firstly, environmental concerns may, in societies where the environment ranks low on political and media agendas, be formulated in political and economic rather than environmental terms. The formulation of environmental concerns in more familiar and successful discursive frames is an attempt to facilitate their acceptance among citizens and their inclusion in the mainstream media, which implies wider public awareness. When presenting demands or describing actions in their digital media output, all the organisations under study utilised political and economic, rather than environmental, lines of argumentation. The environmental frame was not the preferred way of presenting the protest discursively on activist websites. The activists' attempts to make visible the environmental problems inherent to the pulp industry and forest monoculture, and to contribute to the expansion of public debate on the subject, were kept entirely within political and economic frames in their media output.

Secondly, the structure of the organisation and contextual mobilisation traditions, as well as the age of the activists, play a significant role in determining how digital media are conceived and used, in particular in the case of protest practices that involve social media or other interactive online platforms. The more structured NGOs strove towards the creation of one-way, unique and coordinated content that represented the organisation. These organisations put limits on individual expressions of engagement, in particular those involving interactivity. Individualised and interactive forms of activism tend to flourish, this case suggests, within loosely knit organisations like grassroots movements rather than in highly structured organisations such as established environmental NGOs. The leaderless grassroots movement allowed more room for activists to engage in social media and interactive online platforms, individually and without consulting the organisation. They were positive about participation in social media and different interactive online platforms, although they rarely used them. Age was a defining factor here, as older activists did not feel comfortable engaging openly in social media. To them the social media were unknown terrain which they would enter into without the aide of younger, more knowledgeable activists. Rich mobilisation traditions and practices were enhanced by digital media, not substituted by them, even though Argentina and Uruguay have the best Internet and mobile phone access in Latin America.

Thirdly, the relationship between activists' online media and national news media is linked to the national authorities' positioning on the matter in question, as this has implications for the online output of activists. Uruguayan NGOs did not have access to news media, as these echoed the voice of governmental authorities on the subject of pulp mills and forest monoculture. Instead, the NGOs strove to produce and disseminate information and arguments via digital media channels, this being the only way to reach fellow citizens. On the other hand, members of the grassroots organisation, who benefited from the Argentinean government's positive attitude to the protest, had plenty of opportunities to express themselves in local and national media, mainly about the blockade. In other words, national media were perceived, both by NGOs and by grassroots activists, as the most powerful vehicle for increasing awareness about the protest because a wider range of people could be reached that way than through online, user-generated media. In the absence of mainstream media coverage, in the case of Uruguay, and with only event-related information, in the case of Argentina, the background and contextualising framing of the protest were made available mainly through online activist-generated content. Activists used political and economic arguments rather than environmental ones in their quest to gain public attention where they expected a concrete outcome.

References

Avritzer, Leonardo, *Democracy and the Public Space in Latin America* (Princeton: Princeton University Press, 2002).

Atkinson, Joshua, *Alternative Media and Politics of Resistance a Communication Perspective* (New York: Lang, 2010).

Atton, Chris, *An Alternative Internet: Radical Media, Politics and Creativity* (Edinburgh: Edinburgh University Press, 2004), http://dx.doi.org/10.3366/edinburgh/9780748617692.001.0001

Bailey, Olga, Cammaerts, Bart and Carpentier, Nico, *Understanding Alternative Media* (Maidenhead: McGraw Hill and Open University Press, 2008).

Beck, Ulrich, *Risk Society: Towards a New Modernity* (London: Sage, 1992).

Bennett, Lance, 'Social Movements Beyond Borders: Understanding Two Eras of Transnational Activism', in *Transnational Protest and Global Activism*, ed. by Donatella della Porta and Sydney Tarrow (Lanham: Rowman & Littlefield, 2005).

—, and Segerberg, Alexandra, 'Digital Media and the Personalization of Collective Action', *Information, Communication & Society*, 4(6) (2011), 770–799, http://dx.doi.org/10.1080/1369118x.2011.579141

—, and Segerberg, Alexandra, 'The Logic of Connective Action', *Information, Communication & Society*, 15(5) (2012), 739–768, http://dx.doi.org/10.1080/1369118X.2012.670661

Bibolini, Lucia and Baker, Lawrence, '2009 Latin American Telecom Market Forecasts', Report published by BuddeComm, Brazil: Mobile Market — Overview, Statistics & Forecasts, 2009.

Bimber, Bruce, Flanagin, Andrew and Cynthia Stohl, *Collective Action in Organisations: Interaction and Engagement in an Era of Technological Change* (Cambridge: Cambridge University Press, 2012), http://dx.doi.org/10.1017/cbo9780511978777

Calderón Gutiérrez, Fernando, *La protesta social en América Latina*, Cuaderno de Prospectiva Política 1 (Buenos Aires: Siglo Veintiuno, 2012).

Carroll, William C., and Hackett, Robert A., 'Democratic Media Activism through the Lens of Social Movement Theory', *Media Culture and Society* 28(1) (2006), 83–104, http://dx.doi.org/10.1177/0163443706059289

Castells, Manuel, *Communication Power* (Oxford: Oxford University Press, 2009).

Christensen, Christian, 'Discourses of Technology and Liberation: State Aid to Net Activists in an Era of "Twitter Revolutions"', *The Communication Review*, 14(3) (2011), 233–253, http://dx.doi.org/10.1080/10714421.2011.597263

Couldry, Nick, 'Theorizing Media as Practice', *Social Semiotics*, 14(2) (2004), 115–132, http://dx.doi.org/10.1080/1035033042000238295

Cottle, Simon and Lester, Libby, eds., *Transnational Protests and the Media* (New York: Peter Lang, 2011).

Coyer, Kate, Dowmunt, Tony and Fountain, Adam, *The Alternative Media Handbook* (London: Routledge, 2007), http://dx.doi.org/10.4324/9780203821213

Dahlgren, Peter, ed., *Young Citizens and New Media: Learning for Democratic Participation* (New York: Routledge, 2007), http://dx.doi.org/10.4324/9780203941638

De Jong, Wilma, Shaw, Martin and Stammers, Neil, *Global Activism, Global Media* (London: Pluto, 2005), http://soniapsebastiao.weebly.com/uploads/2/0/3/9/20393123/20112012_gcc_e-book_global_activism_global_media.pdf

Downing, John, 'Social Movement Theories and Alternative Media: An Evaluation and Critique', *Communication, Culture and Critique*, 1(1) (2008), 40–50, http://dx.doi.org/10.1111/j.1753-9137.2007.00005.x

Fairclough, Norman, *Critical Discourse Analysis: The Critical Study of Language* (London: Longman, 1995).

Fox, Elizabeth and Waisbord, Silvio, eds., *Latin Politics, Global Media* (Austin: University of Texas Press, 2002).

Hallin, Daniel C. and Papathanassopoulos, Stylianos, 'Political Clientelism and the Media: Southern Europe and Latin America in Comparative Perspective', *Media Culture & Society*, 24 (2002), 175–195, http://dx.doi.org/10.1177/016344370202400202

Kenix, Linda Jean, 'In Search of Utopia: An Analysis of Non-Profit Web Pages', *Information, Communication & Society*, 10(1) (2007), 69–94, http://dx.doi.org/10.1080/13691180701193085

Leistert, Oliver, *From Protest to Surveillance: The Political Rationality of Mobile Media: Modalities of Neoliberalism* (New York: Peter Lang, 2013), http://dx.doi.org/10.3726/978-3-653-03268-0

Leivrouw, Leah, *Alternative and Activist New Media* (Cambridge: Polity, 2011).

MacCaughey, Martha and Ayers, Michael, *Cyberactivism: Online Activism in Theory and Practice* (New York: Routledge, 2003), http://dx.doi.org/10.4324/9780203954317

Melián, Virginia, 'Bridging the Blocked River: A Study on Internet and Mobile Phone Practices within an Environmental Movement Between 2005 and 2008 in Argentina and Uruguay' (Doctoral thesis, Stockholm University, 2012).

Melucci, Alberto, *Challenging Codes: Collective Action in the Information Age* (Cambridge: Cambridge University Press, 1996), http://dx.doi.org/10.1017/CBO9780511520891

Moseley, Mason and Layton, Mathew, 'Prosperity and Protest in Brazil: The Wave of the Future for Latin America?', *Americas Barometer Insights*, 93 (2013), pp. 1–9.

Morozov, Eugene, *The Net Delusion: How the Press Covers Science and Technology* (London: Allen Lane, 2011).

Pakkasvirta, Jussi, 'From Pulp to Fiction? Fray Bentos Pulp Investment Conflict through the Finnish Media', *Cooperation and Conflict*, 43(4) (2008), 421–446, http://dx.doi.org/10.1177/0010836708096883

Papacharissi, Zizi, 'Democracy Online: Civility, Politeness and the Democratic Potential of Online Political Discussion Groups', *New Media & Society*, 6(2) (2004), 259–283, http://dx.doi.org/10.1177/1461444804041444

—, *A Private Sphere: Democracy in a Digital Age* (Cambridge: Polity, 2010).

Rauch, Jennifer, 'Activists as Interpretative Communities: Rituals of Consumption and Interaction in an Alternative Media Audience', *Media, Culture & Society*, 29(6) (2007), 994–1013, http://dx.doi.org/10.1177/0163443707084345

Rodríguez, Clemencia, Ferron, Benjamin and Shamas, Kristin, 'Four Challenges in the Field of Alternative, Radical and Citizens' Media Research', *Media, Culture & Society*, 36(2) (2014), 150–166, http://dx.doi.org/10.1177/0163443714523877

Rockwell, Rick and Janus, Noreene, *Media Power in Central America* (Urbana: University of Illinois Press, 2003).

Shirky, Clay 'The Political Power of Social Media: Technology, The Public Sphere and Political Change', *Foreign Affairs, Council of Foreign Relations* (2011), http://www.foreignaffairs.com/articles/67038/clay-shirky/the-political-power-of-social-media

Silverman, David, *Interpreting Qualitative Data: Methods for Analysing Talk, Text and Interaction* (London: Sage, 2006).

Stein, Laura, 'Social Movement Web Use in Theory and Practice: A Content Analysis of US Movement Websites', *Media, Culture & Society*, 11(5) (2009), 749–771, http://dx.doi.org/10.1177/1461444809105350

—, 'Environmental Website Production: A Structuration Approach', *Media, Culture & Society*, 33(3) (2011), 363–384, http://dx.doi.org/10.1177/0163443710394898

Sveningsson, Malin, Lövheim, Mia and Bergquist, Magnus, *Att Fånga Nättet: Kvalitativa Metoder för Internetforskning* (Lund: Studentliterratur, 2003).

Treré, Emiliano, 'Social Movements as Information Ecologies: Exploring the Co-Evolution of Multiple Internet Technologies for Activism', *Journal of International Communication*, 6 (2012), 2359–2377.

Van de Donk, Win, Loader, Brian D., Nixon, Paul G. and Rucht, Dieter, *Cyberprotest: New Media, Citizens and Social Movements* (London: Routledge, 2004), http://dx.doi.org/10.4324/9780203644225

Valenzuela, Sebastián, Arrigada, Arturo and Scherman Andrés, 'The Social Media Basis of Youth Protest Behaviour: The Case of Chile', *Journal of Communication*, 62 (2012), pp. 299–314, http://dx.doi.org/10.1111/j.1460-2466.2012.01635.x

Villi, Mikko, 'Visual Mobile Communication: Camera Phone Photo Messages as Ritual Communication and Mediated Presence' (Doctoral thesis, Aalto University, 2011).

Waisbord, Silvio, *Watchdog Journalism in South America: News, Accountability, and Democracy* (New York: Columbia University Press, 2000).

Waisbord, Silvio and Peruzzotti, Enrique, 'The Environmental Story that Wasn't: Advocacy, Journalism and the Asambleísmo Movement in Argentina', *Media, Culture & Society*, 31(5) (2009), 142–165, http://dx.doi.org/10.1177/0163443709339462

Waters, Richard D., Burnett, Emily, Lamm, Anna and Lucas, Jessica, 'Engaging Stakeholders through Social Networking: How Non-profit Organisations are Using Facebook', *Public Relations Review*, 35 (2009), 102–106, http://dx.doi.org/10.1016/j.pubrev.2009.01.006

Welp, Yanina and Wheatley, Jonathan, 'The Uses of Digital Media for Contentious Politics in Latin America', in *Digital Media and Political Engagement Worldwide: A Comparative Study*, ed. by Eva Anduiza, Michael James Jensen and Laia Jorba (Cambridge: Cambridge University Press, 2012), http://dx.doi.org/10.1017/cbo9781139108881.010

Yin, Robert K., *Case Study Research: Design and Methods* (Thousand Oaks: Sage, 2003).

3. Exploitation or Preservation? Your Choice! Digital Modes of Expressing Perceptions of Nature and the Land[1]

Coppélie Cocq

This chapter examines the role played by participatory media in environmental activism. The starting point for this study is the current debate on the exploitation of natural resources in Sweden's Sámi region. When discussing this issue, different points of view about the environment are expressed. Some commentators believe that nature should be viewed as a commodity, while others perceive it as a heritage that must be protected. These views are expressed during demonstrations and in newspaper articles. They also circulate online in, for instance, Facebook groups, on Twitter, and through various blogs and YouTube uploads. They are articulated in posts and comments and voiced through music, short films, pictures, and posters. This chapter focussed on YouTube video clips, shedding light on how those who oppose mining depict nature and make their contribution to the environmental debate.

Perceptions of the environment differ according to cultural and social background. Sometimes nature is perceived as a commodity, something to be consumed. Sometimes it is seen as a heritage to preserve. As became evident in interviews conducted in a previous project,[2] perceptions

---

1   The research for this paper was financially supported by the Swedish Foundation for Humanities and Social Sciences, Riksbankens Jubileumsfond.
2   Andersson and Cocq, 'Nature Narrated. A Study of Oral Narratives about Environmental and Natural Disasters from a Folkloristic and Linguistic Ethnographic Perspective', 2012–2014.

http://dx.doi.org/10.11647/OBP.0096.03

of nature and landscape, and an intimate relationship to the land, are experiences that are difficult to convey in words (Cocq 2014a, 2014b). This sense of ineffability is confirmed by the central role played by cultural workers in the debate about the Sámi land exploitation situation. Through fine arts, music, and performance, artists and cultural workers take a stance in the debate, adopting an indigenous, emic perspective. These initiatives contribute to the debate by raising questions about the rights of indigenous people, and by increasing the visibility of Sámi groups in rural areas.

This chapter will explore how visual and audiovisual participatory media can express, shape, and convey perceptions and understanding of nature — that is, perspectives that are difficult to communicate verbally in the public debate on environment and its exploitation. The study focuses on the relationship between media, culture, and society rather than on the use of media for the communication of meaning.

The increasing need to communicate emic perspectives on environmental and indigenous issues is met, and becomes visible through, an increased use of social and participatory media in, among other things, social movements. In contrast to traditional mass media, social media platforms are said to provide 'prosumers' (Olin-Scheller and Wikström 2010; Bruns 2008) due to easier modes of production, diffusion, and consumption.

The potential of social media for enabling marginalised voices to reach arenas they would otherwise not have access is the subject of much debate. As Saskia Sassen (2004) pertinently emphasises, social media are not isolated from social logic. Discourses of democratisation nuance the effects of new media on any larger political debate (O'Neil 2014). Critical voices suggest that social media, in fact, contribute to maintaining or even strengthening existing structures and power relations (Dean 2003; Fuchs 2010).

This study investigates how marginalised voices search for a venue in the media landscape. The case used as an example is that of the environmental movement's resistance to the mining industry's plans for the territory known as Sápmi. The movement is both local — it is concerned with Sápmi, the traditional area of the indigenous people of Europe — and global, insofar as it concerns indigenous rights and environmental struggle.

Mining Boom, Land Rights, and Perceptions of the Environment

Sápmi, the traditional area of Sámi settlement, comprises the northern regions of Sweden, Norway, Finland, and Russia. It is a heterogeneous area in terms of languages, livelihoods, and population. Discourses of decolonisation, cultural and linguistic revitalisation, and mobilisation for strengthening indigenous land rights are topics of immediate interest in contemporary Sápmi. In Sweden, this discourse is becoming increasingly prominent at the national level.

An increasing number of permits for exploration for minerals in Sweden has led to a 'mining boom'. This, in combination with multiple types of exploitation (wind power, etc.) located in reindeer-herding areas, has led to a growing debate about the Swedish Minerals Act, as well as issues such as traditional land use, indigenous rights, mining, and growth in relation to what is termed majority society.

The summer of 2013 was a milestone for the mining resistance movement. That was when reindeer herders, various local actors, environmentalists, and others worked together to prevent a foreign exploration company from conducting exploratory drilling in Gállok (Jokkmokk municipality). From July to September 2013, a group of activists occupied the area in order to block the way for vehicles attempting to enter the prospection area. On several occasions there were confrontations with the police. Through demonstrations, art installations, and debates in social media, the protest movement brought national and international attention to the Gállok events.

Cultural variations in perceptions of the environment have been the subject of previous research. Such variations have been studied in a Sámi context by Rydberg, whose work shows how memories and language link the landscape to the identity of the Sámi in Handölsdalen *sameby* (administrative unit for reindeer herding; Rydberg 2011, 91–93). Conflicts between indigenous groups and international commercial interests elsewhere in the world have also been discussed, in terms of the spillover effects of globalization (e.g., Tsing 2005).

Previous research has also emphasised the need for the investigation of environmental issues in relation to human practices, representations, and behaviour (Nye et al. 2013; Evernden 1992) as well as ecological ethics (Plumwood 2002). The approach to *nature* as a construct and the rejection of the human-nature dichotomy open up the investigation of our practices, narratives, and understandings of the environment as modes of shaping, maintaining, and questioning representations.

Internet videos make it possible to combine different media materials. They disseminate images and movies — along with lyrics and music. This form of digital expression provides new tools that are being used strategically in activist movements. Social media have become a natural channel for activism, and the Web 2.0 has enabled increased communication, commitment, and coordination in activism. The effort to achieve ideological homogeneity is not the most interesting part of this development, but rather the efforts toward dialogue and understanding (Dahlberg 2007).

YouTube: A Channel for Environmental Activism

In order to investigate the use of participatory media in communicating nature, I have chosen two short films on YouTube as case studies. These films circulated in the summer of 2013, at the time of the Gállok conflict. YouTube was the platform that was used to publish videos and give an account of the ongoing struggle, for instance during interventions and clashes with the police. As part of the campaign against the mining industry, short clips were produced and published on YouTube.

The first YouTube video that concerns us was produced under the YouTube account name 'whatlocalpeople'. 'What local people?' is the question that Clive Sinclair-Poulton, president of the British mining company, Beowulf Mining, asked at a presentation of one of its mining projects. The local people that he referred to, or rather questioned the existence of, were the people living in the area of Gállok (Kallak), located 45 kilometres outside Jokkmokk. Sinclair-Poulton's question was rhetorical, and came as a response to a query about possible objections from the local population to a mining project.

The answer to Sinclair-Poulton's statement came partly in the form of a website, http://www.whatlocalpeople.se. When we enter the website, we are met by a short movie showing Sinclair-Poulton's presentation and statement, reinforced by a picture of clear-cutting (a forestry practice in which most or all trees are cut down within a given tract of forest). His question, 'What local people?' is followed, on the website, by an answer in the form of a series of portrait photographs — the faces of the people who live and work in the area, along with the text 'We are the locals!'

Furthermore, the homepage contains tabs with which the web-visitor can navigate and find information about several mining projects in Sápmi. Under the tab 'Vi finns' [We exist], we learn about the website's background:

> The background for the creation of this website was anger. An anger caused by a statement made during an international mining conference in Stockholm. There, representatives of Beowulf Mining (Jokkmokk Iron Mines AB) presented their plans for mining of iron ore in an approximately 4.5 × 5 km large open pit in Gállokjávrre (known as Kallak), 50 kilometres west of Jokkmokk.[3]

Black and white photos are displayed at the head of the webpage — faces that demonstrate the existence of local people, satirising the manner in which Sinclair-Poulton used clear-cutting to illustrate the absence of a local population. The images used here emphasise the statement 'Vi finns!' [We exist]. 'What local people' is also the name of an exhibition, a YouTube account, and has become a slogan in the fight against exploration in the area around Gállok. It is also the title of a spoken-word poem by the artist Mimie Märak, performed at the site of Gállok.[4]

The video *Vägvalet — för fast mark och rent vatten*[5] [*Choice at the crossroads — for solid ground and clean water*], the first example discussed in this chapter, was published by the whatlocalpeople account on 3 July 2013. The video does not mention any specific producer; it simply refers to the movement 'whatlocalpeople'. This was at the beginning of the Gállok occupation, before the events got the attention of local, national, or international media. Almost two years later, the video again circulated in social media forums: on 13 February 2015, a post in the Facebook group Gruvfritt Jokkmokk [Mine-free Jokkmokk] linked to the video, maintaining that it was still of great interest, given the recent resolution from Sweden's Mining Inspectorate referring the final decision on the Gállok mine project to the government.

Other YouTube video materials by whatlocalpeople include records of performances, speeches held at festivals, and demonstrations. Not

---

3   http://www.whatlocalpeople.se/vi-finns [my translation].
4   https://www.youtube.com/watch?v=JiFcEvjIG8w
5   http://www.youtube.com/watch?v=adJDdTw5AsQ

least, it is this account that posted videos of confrontations with the police during the summer of 2013 in Gállok.[6] These are the videos that attract the most viewers.

A short text introduces *Vägvalet*, a 2.30 minute long video:

> En underbar värld eller feta nackars välde. Miljöbalk mot mineralstrategi. Vad väljer du?' [A wonderful world or the empire of the 'fat necks'. Environmental code against mineral strategy. What do you choose?]

> Bli en del av den växande rörelsen [Become part of a growing movement]:
> www.urbergsgruppen.se
> www.whatlocalpeople.se
> www.facebook.com/groups/ingagruvor
> #Kallak

The clip starts with a quote from Dag Hammarskjöld, United Nations Secretary-General from 1953 to 1961 and a Swedish diplomat.

> 'Din skyldighet är "att". Du kan aldrig rädda dig genom "att icke".'
> ['Your duty is "to". You can never save yourself by "to not".']

The clip is introduced by the first two verses of the song 'What a Wonderful World' by Louis Armstrong. Images of forests, flowers and plants, mountain landscapes, birds, moose, and water are displayed on the screen. A banner at the bottom provides information about the Swedish Environmental Code (1998, 808), sustainability, and our responsibility to 'administer nature'.

Fig. 3.1 Screenshot from *Vägvalet* (http://www.youtube.com/watch?v=adJDdTw5AsQ)

---

6   For instance: https://www.youtube.com/watch?v=5Ry06RncwYI; https://www.youtube.com/watch?v=YhhFdLvPinU

Images of unpopulated natural areas are combined with the music to give a sense of harmony. About one minute into the movie, a voice interrupts Armstrong and the slideshow by shouting 'Hallå?! Hallå?!'. This marks the beginning of the second part of the video. The music changes to the song 'Staten och kapitalet' ['State and capital'] by the Swedish punk band Ebba Grön. This gives the slideshow a different tone. A banner with the text 'test pit at Gállok (Kallak) July 1, 2013' provides information about the images displayed, including a video of a great trench dug through the forest by machines. The text at the bottom of the screen now concerns the global demand for minerals. Headlines of news articles about the mining industry and its profits are shown in a collage, followed by images of machines and wide tracks dug into the ground, as well as of representatives of the government and the mining industry. Headlines of news articles appear again, this time referring to a possible environmental disaster, followed by pictures of an open mining pit.

The video ends with the words: 'You can choose — your children and grandchildren cannot'. 'Be part of an emerging/growing movement' appears, with links to websites and Facebook groups. In the background, we hear voices shouting, as they do at demonstrations: 'No mines in Jokkmokk'. In the last image, a text reads, 'We believe in the future'.

Fig. 3.2 Screenshot from *Vägvalet* (http://www.youtube.com/watch?v=adJDdTw5AsQ)

The video is divided into two parts, each representing contrasting and conflicting descriptions of the environment. The first illustrates the values of sustainability and responsibility, reinforced by text about the Swedish Environmental Code. The images connote harmony, showing wildlife, pristine nature, etc. The music is meant to reinforce the frame of harmony, hope, and celebration of life and the world. The video's aesthetics anthropomorphise nature. This is a recurrent rhetorical strategy used in environmental discourse that has been proven effective in influencing people's relation to nature, fostering conservation behaviour, and enhancing connectedness to nature (Tam et al. 2013).

The video's second part stands in contrast to this, not least because of the abrupt break and change in the tone of images and sound. The focus is now on financial gain and the risks run by environment and population. The pictures show traces left in the landscape and images of politicians and mining companies. The music, the lyrics of which make a statement about government and capitalism, aims at inspiring anger. The voice heard at the beginning of the Ebba Grön song, which interrupts the middle of the film, functions as a wake-up call. The two perspectives are set out in contrast, placed next to each other in order to offer the viewer a choice: the one or the other. The title indicates that we have reached a 'crossroads' and that this is about the future ('your children and grandchildren').

The second video considered here is entitled *Our land, our water, our future.*[7] It was produced and published by the photographer Tor Lundberg Tuorda on 19 December 2012. He has produced and published several videos on YouTube on the topics of the mining boom, the preservation of the environment, and responses to and actions against colonialism. He participates regularly in events related to the mining boom, including protest marches, and meetings. Tor Lundberg Tuorda is also active in academic circles. In an interview, he explains his work and the ambition behind his films:

> The only thing I can do is to inform, to be stubborn. There is so much total madness in this. That's what I do, it is the only power I have — with my camera as a weapon.[8]

Other films by Lundberg Tuorda include the recent 'The Parasite',[9] about Swedish colonisation. His works have been screened in various contexts. His short film *Mineralernas förbannelse* [*The Curse of Minerals*] has, for instance, been shown as part of the museum exhibition 'Inland'[10] at the Västerbotten Museum in 2015.

---

7   http://www.youtube.com/watch?v=5p6BygBUmGA
8   Personal interview, 30 May 2013.
9   https://www.youtube.com/watch?v=IYM3grMxYJs, published on 23 January 2015.
10   http://www.inland.nu

The video *Our land, our water, our future* is a 1:54-long English-language clip introduced with the words: 'This video was shown in Stockholm 17/11 at [2012] at the manifestation "Our land, Our water, Our Future" (© Tor Lundberg)'.

Our land, our water, our future is composed of stills and moving pictures. The images depict water, a child drinking out of a *guksi* (Sámi drinking vessel of birch wood), a person swimming in a lake, a reindeer herd in a snow landscape, a child making a snow angel, animals in the forests. A female voice accompanies the video declaims: 'Clean water, fresh air, white snow, deep forests. This is where we come from. This is what we live off'. As the voice continues speaking, the film shows people picking berries and herbs, hunting, fishing, boiling water over an open fire, cooking and eating outdoors, all activities that are in harmony with nature, that use natural resources, and that involve children.

Fig. 3.3 Screenshot from *Our Land* (http://www.youtube.com/watch?v=5p6BygBUmGA)

A shift occurs in the story, however, when the voice says:

> Now, [the] mining industry threatens to destroy our lands. Companies from all over the world want to convert the natural wealth into money. They leave only devastated mountains, forests and rivers behind: an impoverished future for our children.

At 0:57 in the film, a picture of Ruovddevárre, located in the Laponia World Heritage Area, appears along with the text 'Owned by English Beowulf Mining' — that is, the British company prospecting in Gállok. While the view zooms in on the mountain, we hear the sound of an explosion. The mountain and trees tremble. Next, we see a photo of

Sarek National Park, the world heritage area of Laponia, while hearing the sound of an airplane in the background. A text reads: 'Ore-searching by the Swedish State. Bårddetjåhkkå, Sarek national park'.

Fig. 3.4 Screenshot from *Our Land* (http://www.youtube.com/watch?v=5p6BygBUmGA)

Following that is a picture with the text 'Gállok (Kallak) owned by English Beowulf mining'. Here again, we hear the sound of ongoing blasting. A hole emerges in the middle of the picture that expands to another photo: one of a mine (an open pit). The forests and mountains are erased by the mine, illustrating what Gállok would look like if a mine were to be built there.

Fig. 3.5 Screenshot from *Our Land* (http://www.youtube.com/watch?v=5p6BygBUmGA)

The loud noise of machines takes over and the frame suddenly becomes a dark screen. The voice comes back, asking 'Is this what we need? Is this what we want?'. The video concludes with brief information about the producer.

This video is built as a story that begins with humans in harmony with nature. The natural resources are berries, game, fish, etc. A complication in the narrative occurs when the mining industry comes into the picture. In the second part of the story, the harmony is disrupted. This disruption is visualised through the blurring of images, trembling, and noises. The end of the story is uncertain. The narrative voice turns back to the audience, sharing the concern depicted in the film, as well as a sense of responsibility.

Contesting Narratives

The two short films presented above produce two parallel discourses about the environment. These discourses stand out by virtue of their contrast, which establishes them as mutually exclusive. One discourse focuses on sustainability, harmony between humans and nature, and a long-term perspective. The other focuses on exploitation (mining) and how it affects the landscape. The portrayal of an exploitative attitude's effects on the environment amounts to a portrayal of devastation which reinforces the idea of preservation suggested in the first discourse.

Although these ways to represent the environment stand in contrast to each other, they are presented from the same perspective. Traditional use of the environment and traditional interaction with the land and the landscape are core values. Other uses and interactions, an open pit for instance, are associated with devastation.

The articulation of the two conflicting discourses on the environment does not suggest a dialogue between the two different representations. When it comes to communication, these films are concerned with communicating one perception of the environment, that of the protest movement opposed to the mining industry; they do not communicate the discourses of the pro-mining movement.[11]

---

11 A study of how nature is communicated by the pro-mining advocates is not included in this chapter.

Bringing into question the existence of local people, exemplified by the statement of Clive Sinclair-Poulton, transforms Gállok into a 'terra nullius' (Fitzmaurice 2007), an unoccupied area belonging to no one. This discourse legitimises exploitation of the area. It also justifies the area's use as a potential solution to the shortage of jobs and an increasing need for minerals (cf. Frost 1981).

The question 'what local people?' is therefore a strong rhetorical position. It does more than question the presence of a local population and local rights to land and water. Those who feel a strong connection to that particular place find their identity and existence questioned. The short films described in this chapter can be interpreted as a response, an effort to increase the visibility of people in the Sápmi region. The films and stills show locals (presumably) in interaction with nature — not a *terra nullius*. Human presence in the landscape is almost exclusively represented by local people. The 'others' are machines, represented here by an airplane, digging machines, and other heavy equipment. Politicians and leaders from the mining industry are not present on site; they appear in excerpts from the media's coverage. The human presence involved in the area's exploitation is, accordingly, toned down and hidden behind machines. This creates a dehumanisation of the mining industry that in itself produces a contrast with the anthropomorphism of nature illustrated in the first part of each video.

Both videos make use of rhetorical techniques to include the audience. The online visitor is not addressed as a passive viewer: at the end of each video, the audience is asked 'Is this what we need? Is this what we want?', and is reminded that 'You can choose — your children and grandchildren cannot'. The use of 'we' and 'you' explicitly addresses the person watching the video. Thus, the audience is asked to take a side when faced with the two contrasting views of nature and the environment. The use of pronouns such as 'we' and 'our', however, does not only serve to include the audience. They also express a sense of possessiveness. Still more directly, the question of responsibility is addressed — that is, the mining industry's and politicians' irresponsibility. At the end of each of the short films, the question is turned back to the viewer: what is YOUR choice? Take a stand! — that is to say, assume responsibility.

The videos give an illusion of interaction: 'you' can choose how the narrative will continue, how it will end. The course of the film is determined, but what will happen next is indeterminate. In *Vägvalet*, we are invited to contribute to developing the narrative towards a harmonic interplay between humans and nature, by agreeing to 'join the movement'.

Media Logic

'Activist media' (Lievrouw 2011) set themselves apart from traditional communication by being different channels rather than different forms of communication. As has been emphasised in other studies (Altheide 2013), the conceptual logic remains unchanged across media. This media logic is 'a form of communication and the process through which media transmit and communicate information' (Altheide 2013, 225). The video clips are examples of tools for communicating points of view and perceptions of nature. They are not isolated; their context, i.e., their origin in activist movements and reactions to prospections in Gállok and in Sápmi, is formed not only by the contemporary debate about the environment and indigenous rights, but also by the media landscape from which they emerge, as well as by a social logic composed by power structures and authorities.

The debate links together different networks of alternative and marginalised voices, authorities and elites. In the videos, one can discern the following networks: Sámi reindeer herders, other locals, environmental activists — through reference to the demonstration in Stockholm — politicians, and the mining industry. Authority and power relations are expressed in the positions given to the actors. Politicians are viewed in settings that denote authority, such as political meetings and conferences. Locals, on the other hand, are portrayed as isolated from larger social contexts, but in their home environment, illustrating traditional knowledge and emic understanding — which also lends authority.

The offline context in which the YouTube clips emerged is yet another aspect to be taken into account. The film by Tor Lundberg Tuorda, for instance, was shown at a demonstration. Tuorda and whatlocalpeople (as a YouTube account and a catch phrase) are closely associated with the coverage of the events of Gállok in the summer of 2013. At that time, neither local nor national media were covering the conflict. The first police actions at the site would have taken place unnoticed had it not been for the cameras and smartphones of activists and locals. Amateur films were posted on YouTube and photos were shared on social media forums, eventually attracting the attention of international and, subsequently, Swedish media.

The issue of exploitation and land rights has, since then, attracted the attention of the mass media and been the topic of several articles in international, national, and local newspapers. It has been the subject of books (Müller 2013; Müller 2015; Tidholm 2012) and national and international television documentaries. Before such attention, the topic was rarely discussed in media or touched upon in public discourse. Emic perspectives were marginalised. Today, even though locals and environmentalists have succeeded in making their voices heard in the mass media, neither these media nor public discourse sufficiently reflect the variety of perspectives on the issue.

The video clips discussed in this chapter operate within the context of a debate about exploitation in Sápmi. They borrow elements from media and political discourses, from demonstrations, and from activism. This entwinement and interplay between the videos and the social logic of the debate illustrate the 'new social condition' defined as mediatization, where 'the media may no longer be conceived as being separate from social and cultural institutions' (Hjarvard 2013).

The clips make use of principles of form, language, and aesthetics borrowed from other media. Depictions of nature as harmonious, quiet, and rich have connotations similar to those found in advertisements promoting biological products or tourist brochures, for instance. But the videos also copy other media, such as traditional media news channels: the banner at the bottom of the screen, with its informative text, and the chaotic pictures (movement, sound) bring to mind reports from conflict areas. The voice that interrupts Louis Armstrong in *Vägvalet* suggests a reporter trying to make us pay attention to a live report from the field, thus creating an impression of immediacy.

In terms of affordance and usability (Norman 1999), YouTube facilitates the diffusion of the videos, which can be posted or linked to on other social media platforms — common sharing practices that can result in a quick, free, and large-scale dissemination of information. The short format of the videos and the fact that information about the legislation (the Environmental Code) is given in an accessible way — devoid of legal jargon — also increases the videos' usability.

Mediatization and media logic imply that short films, such as those studied here, create and are forced into a mode of communication that is familiar, appealing, and recognisable in terms of language and framing. The format of the films makes it apparent that they were produced with limited resources. Thus, even an uninformed viewer would rapidly recognise these videos as the products of activists rather than as the products of the mining industry or a lobby organisation. In a polarised debate such as this one, the 'home-made', DIY aspect lends credibility and authenticity to the message that the video clips convey.

The choice of aesthetics, language, and principles of form indicates that the producers prefer to communicate according to the logic and mechanism typical of activist movements, rather than adopt the system mechanisms used by professionals. The media logic of activist media prevails here. This implies that the videos address an audience that recognises and is receptive to this particular logic. Interestingly, although the DIY aspect of these activist initiatives is manifest in the format, some aspects are, on the other hand, 'borrowed' from traditional media (the banner, the speaker voice) — as discussed above.

The music in the short videos is another vehicle for perspectives, ideologies, and identities. 'What a Wonderful World' and the soundtrack of *Our land* reinforce the sense of harmony expressed in the photos and moving pictures. The song *Staten och kapitalet* in the second part of *Vägvalet*, an anti-capitalist critique of the relation of the state to capitalist corporations, is a Swedish classic. It was created by the Progg-band[12] Blå tåget [Blue Train] in 1972. The version used in the video is a cover from 1980s by the Swedish punk band Ebba Grön. The choice of the song in itself conveys an ideology and a message (Arvidsson 2008). Re-emerging in a new context, the song carries power and resonance from the original context (Frandy 2013), creating continuity between anti-capitalist movements of the 1970s and environmental activism in 2013.

The familiar narrative structure of the videos contributes to their affordance. The narratives of the two clips are similar and follow a structure recognisable from oral genres. Borrowing terminology from narrative research (Labov and Waletzky 1967), we can describe this

---

12 Progg was a left-wing, anti-commercial musical movement in Sweden in the late 1960s and 1970s.

structure as consisting of various phases, including an abstract (an introduction to what the story is about, that is, the traditional use of the land), an orientation (the main actors are local people, the story takes place in Sápmi, in our time), and a complicating action (exploitation). The next phase, the evaluation, tells us about the threats and dangers that arise. The concluding phases (result and coda) are not provided; the story remains incomplete and the viewer is addressed directly, encouraged to influence the final outcome. The course of action is simplified and the actors are depicted, crudely, as good and peaceful or bad and aggressive. Nature is anthropomorphised, while the workers of the mining companies are left out, with the focus being on technique and infrastructure.

Due to the format and the context of the production of short films, it is a challenge to present the complexity of the situation. To some extent, the narratives illustrated in *Vägvalet* and *Our land* fail in representing the many actors, the variety of perspectives, the various conditions, and the geographical specificity of different mining projects at play in the debate over exploitation in Sápmi. On the other hand, communicating a message concerning the environment in the format of a short video in participatory media inherently implies and requires a degree of simplification. This is the case in the videos meant to reach out and illustrate the impact of mining in Sápmi.

The anonymous producer(s) of the whatlocalpeople homepage and user of the YouTube account of that same name both stress the utility of participatory media as a benefit. 'It is a good way to convey a message, by linking […] One can quickly get a knock-on effect'.[13] The producer also mentioned the opportunity to be thought-provoking without forcing an interpretation on people. 'One must make people think, not make things too easy for them — let them put two and two together'.

To achieve this, the producer uses pictures and films, 'as a complement to text. It can be tiresome to read a compendium. But with pictures, one can create interest in reading that compendium. Like the pictures in opinion pieces in *DN* [*Dagens Nyheter*, the national newspaper]'.

When it comes to the participatory aspects of these YouTube videos, it is difficult to determine their impact. *Vägvalet* had (as of 18 February 2015) no visible comments on YouTube; it had 944 viewings. *Our land*

---

13   Personal interview, 31 May 2013.

had 493 viewings and 2 comments to the producer (by 18 February 2015). The videos have been spread on Facebook, a platform more welcoming to comments and responses than YouTube. Interaction through comments, in other words, takes place to a greater extent outside the frame of YouTube. Sharing videos on other platforms, such as Facebook, is indeed in itself a mode of interaction. Although it would be relevant to examine the reception of the videos in relation to the producer's intention and ambition to reach an audience, this falls outside of the scope of this chapter.

Polarisation or Zone of Contact

One important question in studies of activism and social media is whether social media can create a zone of contact for increased dialogue between the parties in a conflict, or if, on the contrary, social media contribute to a polarisation of the debate by creating spaces primarily for those who are already in agreement with each other.

In the case of this particular study, there is one aspect that one must keep in mind. The general Swedish population has little knowledge of Sámi culture, history, and living conditions. Lack of knowledge is one factor that might complicate the creation of mutual understanding, leading to a polarisation of the debate. From this perspective, any effort aimed at spreading knowledge and information about Sápmi as a cultural landscape, and about its population, would improve people's understanding of the Sámi perspective on the conflict.

The controversy over mining and exploitation is, however, not only a Sámi issue. It is also an environmental concern, a question of human and indigenous rights. Debates over the opening of new mines are related to specific geographical places. The environment and specific places become common denominators for various groups concerned with the issue — environmentalists, reindeer herders, indigenous rights activists, and locals. The importance of local attachment in framing social movements is articulated in social media. These media play a role in bringing together different groups and interests in activist movements, as happened in the case of the movement against the mining industry. Participatory media are a meeting point where one talks, organises, fetches and spreads information; they facilitate the emergence of networks. From this perspective, social media constitute a zone of contact (cf. Pettersen 2011) for different groups concerned with the same issue.

The question remains, however, whether social media can be a zone of dialogue and exchange for those on opposite sides of a debate.[14] The videos, through their aesthetics and principles of form and language, address an audience receptive to arguments about sustainability, environmental preservation, traditional use of natural resources (fishing, berry picking, etc.), and respect for the natural and cultural landscape. The opposite standpoint is depicted in negative terms, with focus on devastation, destruction, disturbance, and greed. As seen from this perspective, the videos do not invite dialogue. Rather, these examples illustrate how participatory media are used for creating a space for marginalised voices and counter discourses, and for diffusion of information.

The videos also address people who are interested in debating the advantages and disadvantages of the mining project as it relates to the wider issue concerning the exploitation of natural resources. At the very least, the videos might 'make people think', to quote the producer of whatlocalpeople. The videos invite people to take sides. They give information; they communicate a perspective in an effort to convince. To address such a heterogeneous audience is naturally challenging. The videos elaborate a perception of the environment and of the relationship between landscape and people based on a direct, unmediated experience of nature. Part of the audience might very probably be composed of people who have experienced nature in Sápmi only from a distance. Discourses about, and representations of, a landscape from which the actor is distanced tend to reproduce a 'coloniser gaze' (see for instance Jørgensen 2014) as opposed to a local gaze. There is a risk that communicating nature through Internet videos to a broad audience might, thus, create distance to the landscape. The clips are produced from an emic, local perspective, and their context of production (including producers, social context, media logic, and conduits) must necessarily be taken into account if one is to fully

---

14   Without data about the consumption and reception of the YouTube videos, any discussion of their impact on pro-mining advocates would be hazardous.

understand the relationship between the landscape and people that these clips illustrate and shape.

Conclusions

The short videos do more than provide a narrative about the environment. They can also include, reflect, and shape the debate about mining in Sápmi. They illustrate how, for voices in the margin, participatory media open up alternative modes of outreach communication. These can be means for self-representation, in this case they allow the locals to stress their presence in the landscape and their view about what nature is. The circulation of information which YouTube made possible is primarily a diffusion of information in an effort to raise awareness.

The perception of nature and the environment shaped and narrated in the films focuses on harmony and the interaction between people and landscape that results from traditional land use. The way in which nature is depicted is framed by the need to protect the environment and assume responsibility, particularly now when exploitation threatens its existence.

The videos present polarised narratives. Although these narratives represent two differing views on natural resources, they do so from a single perspective. They represent the point of view of people who have a specific agenda, one of many viewpoints expressed during the debate. Other actors, such as local pro-mining movements, are not represented. This simplification of the debate can be understood as partially rhetorical, a consequence of a media logic and mode, influenced by the choice of media. This chapter's analysis of the films indicates that their main target audience are those concerned about issues such as environmental preservation.

It would therefore be hazardous to draw conclusions about the potential of participatory media for opening a dialogue or for preventing conflict. But, less than two years after the publication of the first YouTube videos of the kind discussed here, the topic of the mining boom on indigenous land has moved from the periphery to the centre of public debate. Undeniably, extensive use of YouTube, Facebook, Twitter, and blogs during and after the conflict in Gállok has, at the very least, helped trigger this shift.

References

Altheide, David L., 'Media Logic, Social Control, and Fear', *Communication Theory*, 23(3) (2013), 223–238, http://dx.doi.org/10.1111/comt.12017

Arvidsson, Alf, *Musik Och Politik Hör Ihop: Diskussioner, Ställningstaganden Och Musicerande 1965–1980* (Möklinta: Gidlund, 2008).

Bruns, Axel, *Blogs, Wikipedia, Second Life, and Beyond: From Production to Produsage* (New York: Peter Lang, 2008).

Cocq, Coppélie, 'Kampen Om Gállok. Platsskapande Och Synliggörande', *Kulturella Perspektiv. Svensk Etnologisk Tidskrift*, 23(1) (2014a), 5–12.

—, 'Att Berätta Och återberätta: Intervjuer, Interaktiva Narrativer Och Berättigande', *Kulturella Perspektiv. Svensk Etnologisk Tidskrift*, 23(4) (2014b), 22–29.

Dahlberg, L., 'Rethinking the Fragmentation of the Cyberpublic: From Consensus to Contestation', *New Media & Society*, 9(5) (2007), 827–847, http://dx.doi.org/10.1177/1461444807081228

Dean, Jodi, 'Why the Net Is Not a Public Sphere', *Constellations*, 10(1) (2003), 95–112, http://dx.doi.org/10.1111/1467-8675.00315

Evernden, Lorne Leslie Neil, *The Social Creation of Nature* (Baltimore: Johns Hopkins University Press, 1992).

Fitzmaurice, Andrew, 'The Genealogy of *terra nullius*', *Australian Historical Studies*, 38(129) (2007), 1–15, http://dx.doi.org/10.1080/10314610708601228

Frandy, Tim, 'Revitalization, Radicalization, and Reconstructed Meanings: The Folklore of Resistance During the Wisconsin Uprising', *Western Folklore*, 72(3–4) (2013), 368–391.

Frost, Alan, 'New South Wales as *terra nullius*: The British Denial of Aboriginal Land Rights, *Historical Studies*, 19(77) (1981), 513–523, http://dx.doi.org/10.1080/10314618108595656

Fuchs, C., 'Alternative Media as Critical Media', *European Journal of Social Theory*, 13(2) (2010), 173–192, http://dx.doi.org/10.1177/1368431010362294

Hjarvard, Stig, *The Mediatization of Culture and Society* (New York: Routledge, 2013), http://dx.doi.org/10.4324/9780203155363

Jørgensen, Finn Arne, 'The Armchair Traveler's Guide to Digital Environmental Humanities', *Environmental Humanities*, 4(1) (2014), 95–112, http://dx.doi.org/10.1215/22011919-3614944

Labov, William, and Waletzky, Joshua, 'Narrative Analysis', in *Essays on the Verbal and Visual Arts*, ed. by J. Helm (Seattle and London: University of Washington Press, 1967), pp. 12–44, http://www.ling.upenn.edu/~rnoyer/courses/103/narrative.pdf

Lievrouw, Leah, *Alternative and Activist New Media* (Cambridge: Polity, 2011).

Müller, Arne, *Smutsiga Miljarder. Den Svenska Gruvboomens Baksida* (Skellefteå: Ord & Visor, 2013).

—, *Norrlandsparadoxen — En Utvecklingsdröm Med Problem* (Skellefteå: Ord & Visor, 2015).

Norman, Donald, 'Affordance, Conventions and Design', *Interactions*, 6(3) (1999), 38–43, http://dx.doi.org/10.1145/301153.301168

Nye, David E., Rugg, Linda, Fleming, James and Emmet, Robert, 'The Emergence of the Environmental Humanities' (2013), http://www.mistra.org/download/18.7331038f13e40191ba5a23/Mistra_Environmental_Humanities_May2013.pdf

O'Neil, Mathieu, 'Hacking Weber: Legitimacy, Critique, and Trust in Peer Production', *Information, Communication & Society*, 17(7) (2014), 872–888, http://dx.doi.org/10.1080/1369118x.2013.850525

Olin-Scheller, Christina, and Wikström, Patrik, 'Literary Prosumers: Young People's Reading and Writing in a New Media Landscape', *Education Inquiry*, 11 (2010), 41–56, http://dx.doi.org/10.3402/edui.v1i1.21931

Pettersen, Bjørg, 'Mind the Digital Gap: Questions and Possible Solutions for Design of Databases and Information Systems for Sámi Traditional Knowledge', *Dieđut* 1 (2011), 163–192.

Plumwood, Val, *Environmental Culture: The Ecological Crisis of Reason* (London: Routledge, 2002).

Rydberg, Tomas, *Landskap, territorium och identitet — exemplet Handölsdalens sameby (Landscape, territory and identity — examples Handöldalens Sami village). Kulturgeografiska institutionen. Forskarskolan I Geografi* (Uppsala: Uppsala universitet, 2011), http://www.diva-portal.org/smash/get/diva2:413828/FULLTEXT01.pdf

Sassen, Saskia, 'Local Actors in Global Politics', *Current Sociology*, 52(4) (2004), 649–670, http://dx.doi.org/10.1177/0011392104043495

Swedish Environmental Code, SFS 1998:808 (Stockholm: Ministry of the Environment and Energy, 1998), http://www.government.se/contentassets/be5e4d4ebdb4499f8d6365720ae68724/the-swedish-environmental-code-ds-200061

Tam, Kim-Pong, Lee, Sau-Lai and Chao, Melody Manchi, 'Saving Mr. Nature: Anthropomorphism Enhances Connectedness to and Protectiveness toward Nature', *Journal of Experimental Social Psychology*, 49 (2013), 514–521, http://dx.doi.org/10.1016/j.jesp.2013.02.001

Tidholm, Po, *Norrland: Essäer Och Reportage* (Luleå: Teg Publishing, 2012).

Tsing, Anna Lowenhaupt. *Friction: An Ethnography of Global Connection* (Princeton: Princeton University Press, 2005).

Internet resources

Videos by Tor Lundberg Tuorda:

Our Land, http://www.youtube.com/watch?v=5p6BygBUmGA

The Parasite, https://www.youtube.com/watch?v=IYM3grMxYJs

Videos by Whatlocalpeople:

The Answer https://www.youtube.com/watch?v=-FPeOPTDhio

Poem, https://www.youtube.com/watch?v=JiFcEvjIG8w

Vägvalet, http://www.youtube.com/watch?v=adJDdTw5AsQ

Gruvmotståndet trappas upp i Gállok, dag 1, https://www.youtube.com/watch?v=5Ry06RncwYI

Polisingripande i Kallak, del 3, https://www.youtube.com/watch?v=YhhFdLvPinU

Other resources

Exhibition

Inland, Västerbottens Museum, http://www.inland.nu

Interviews

Tor Lundberg Tuorda (30 May 2013), personal interview.

Producer of Whatlocalpeople (31 May 2013), personal interview.

4. Natural Ecology Meets Media Ecology: Indigenous Climate Change Activists' Views on Nature and Media

Anna Roosvall and Matthew Tegelberg

Introduction

This chapter examines how views on natural ecology connect to specific media ecologies. It focuses particularly on activists in organisations working to highlight indigenous perspectives on climate change and the threat climate change poses to many indigenous communities. Of principal concern is how these activists discuss Traditional Ecological Knowledge (TEK) in relation to mainstream/alternative, national/local and non-indigenous/indigenous news media, in analogue as well as digital forms, and the roles indigenous perspectives play in media ecologies where the activists live.

Ecology refers to the relationship between a group of living things and their environment (Merriam-Webster online). The term is most commonly used in relation to the natural and biological sphere, as in the discussion of climate change as a threat to natural ecosystems. Concurrently, there is a tradition in media research that views media as environments in a similar way (Scolari 2013). Much like the diverse flora and fauna that make up any natural ecosystem, media ecologies consist of different forms of media (mainstream, alternative, national, local, online, and offline) and media actors (producers, consumers, intermediaries, etc.). Each possesses varying degrees of power and influence within a particular media ecosystem. The case studied in this chapter reveals how natural and media ecosystems are (dis)connected in mediated communication on climate change.

Climate change is a global issue with particular impacts for indigenous peoples, especially those who rely on natural ecosystems as a primary means of subsistence (see Roosvall and Tegelberg 2015). Indigenous peoples often engage closely with land and waters, practicing livelihoods that depend on nature. In Tebtebba's (Indigenous Peoples' International Centre for Policy Research and Education) *Guide on Climate Change and Indigenous Peoples*, Victoria Tauli-Corpuz[1] writes:

> Our ancestors and we, the present generations, have coped and adapted to climate change for thousands of years. However, the magnitude and nature of present-day climate change seriously challenges our resilience and our capacities to adapt. We contributed the least to climate change because of our sustainable traditional livelihoods and lifestyles and yet we are the ones who are heavily impacted by it (2009, vii).

The Tebtebba report details climate change impacts on diverging ecosystems and the indigenous groups who live in these areas: the 'tropical and sub-tropical ecosystems', 'semi-arid and arid lands' (drylands), 'high altitude and high montane ecosystems', 'coastal and marine ecosystem' (small-island states and low-lying areas), and the 'arctic ecosystem'. UN reports have likewise discussed the particular threat climate change poses in certain areas where indigenous groups live. Sámi reindeer husbandry, for instance, is a traditional form of sustenance that is threatened by climate change in relation to the Arctic ecosystem in Sápmi (Sámi land: northern Finland, Norway, Russia, and Sweden) (Anaya 2011). Our previous research found that indigenous peoples and their perspectives on these critical issues were underrepresented in media coverage of climate change (Roosvall and Tegelberg 2012, 2013, 2015). These findings contribute to a wider literature on the misrepresentation and marginalisation of indigenous voices in mainstream public discourses in many countries (Avison

---

1   Victoria Tauli-Corpuz is now United Nations Special Rapporteur on the rights of indigenous peoples. She is an indigenous leader from the Kankanaey Igorot people of the Cordillera Region in the Philippines. She was the chair of the UN Permanent Forum on Indigenous Issues, 2005–2010.

and Meadows 2000; Knudsen 2006; Anderson and Robertson 2011; Pietikäinen 2003, 2008). This in turn can be related to the media ecologies that indigenous peoples feel they must relate to as they try to make their voices heard on these issues (Roosvall and Tegelberg 2015).

Three aspects of these media ecologies are particularly relevant to this chapter: how mainstream and alternative media work separately and relate to each other; how national and local media work separately and relate to each other; and finally how non-indigenous and indigenous media work separately and relate to each other, which can take place in analogue as well as digital outlets. Mainstream media and alternative media work in different ways, for instance, by citing different sources (Atton 2002; Harcup 2003). This is important for groups, like indigenous peoples, that fall outside of mainstream media sourcing practices (Pietikäinen 2003; Roosvall and Tegelberg 2013, 2015). While sourcing differences can also characterise local media coverage, added distinctions can be made between local and national media (for more on alternative vs. mainstream local media, see Harcup 2003). For instance, there has been a tendency for local journalists to spend less time outside the newsroom, diminishing their encounters with local people more than journalists working for national media (Witschge and Nygren 2009). Another difference is that national media are produced far away from indigenous sites affected by climate change, whereas certain local and regional media are produced closer to these sites. Furthermore, non-indigenous and indigenous media tend to differ in that indigenous media strengthen indigenous identity (Russell 2005; Pietikäinen 2008; Hafsteinsson and Bredin 2010) while non-indigenous media tend to marginalise indigenous peoples (Pietikäinen 2003; Anderson and Robertson 2011).

The categories mentioned frequently overlap so that mainstream media, national media, and non-indigenous media can be used in conjunction to characterise the same media outlets. However, some nations have national indigenous media (e.g., Sweden, Canada). Additional overlap and demarcations can be observed between alternative, local, and indigenous media. While such distinctions and intersections are relevant to this study, we do not intend to map the media systems discussed here. Instead we focus on indigenous activists' general views on media ecology as well as those particular to the countries and/or regions they inhabit. In the interviews (conducted in 2011) we did not make an explicit distinction between analogue and digital or legacy and social media, but focused on mainstream versus alternative media more generally. Distinctions between analogue and digital as well as legacy and social media will come up in this study to the extent that the interviewees themselves bring it up. We take as a point of departure the distinctions mainstream/alternative, and also national/local and indigenous/non-indigenous media, following results from a previous study (Roosvall and Tegelberg 2015) where the same interviews we analyse here pointed to the relevance of these categories. In the current chapter, we elaborate on and explore these findings further within a media ecology framework, with a focus on how natural ecology is represented by the activists and by the media in this context. We emphasise two key themes: how these activists assess media representations of indigenous issues, indigenous knowledge, and TEK; and what strategies the activists employ to overcome the communication challenges these media ecologies pose for them.

Hence the aim of this chapter is to explore how representations of views on natural ecology are related to the constitution of media ecologies. We are particularly interested in indigenous activists' perspectives on these issues in their work to spread knowledge about, and influence public opinion on, the effects of climate change on indigenous lands and the planet at large. In order to address these concerns we consider the following questions:

- How do indigenous actors facing critical ecological problems caused by climate change relate to and assess the media's role in generating awareness of these challenges?

- How are views on natural ecology, and particularly TEK, connected to media ecology, specifically concerning different parts of media ecosystems?

- What types of approaches to climate challenges do interviewees advocate for and how do they envision the media's role in addressing these problems?

The chapter begins by distinguishing between TEK and Western scientific approaches to climate change. It then presents and discusses media ecology theories. This theoretical discussion provides a framework for the analysis of interviews conducted with indigenous activists at the

2011 UN Climate Summit in Durban, South Africa. The activists call for changes to a news media ecosystem that currently marginalises their voices, in particular their critical perspectives on climate change and knowledge of its impact on natural ecosystems. The interviewees stress the importance of further integration of TEK perspectives into the existing news media ecosystem. We conclude that these changes are urgently needed in order to establish a more democratic and effective means of addressing climate change and avoiding fatal changes to our planetary ecosystems.

Defining Traditional Ecological Knowledge

Traditional Ecological Knowledge is one of the phrases used to identify the environmental knowledge and cultural subsistence practices of indigenous peoples (Eriksen and Adams 2010). Indigenous particularity is sometimes emphasised in the terminology itself, in phrases like 'indigenous environmental knowledge' (ibid.). We have chosen to use the term Traditional Ecological Knowledge (TEK) since it recognises the existence of this type of knowledge among indigenous peoples, while not exclusively limiting it to these groups. Definitions of TEK, however, tend to differ according to the worldviews of those who define it (McGregor 2002). In Western thought, TEK is frequently conceptualised as knowledge that exists in a domain separate from the people who possess it. For indigenous peoples, TEK may instead encompass nature, culture, and spirituality: 'Focus is on *relationships* between knowledge, people, and all of Creation (the "natural" world as well as the spiritual)' (McGregor 2002, 8). This relational approach often influences how indigenous peoples relate to and make use of natural resources. Gunvor Guttorm (2011, 69–70) highlights, in a similar way, how the TEK of indigenous Sámi in Sweden is differentiated from other local knowledge in the same region. The main difference being that the indigenous variant includes a spiritual take on the idea that humans are part of nature. Nature, culture, and spirituality intersect in a similar way in, for instance, indigenous Andean worldviews (Apffel-Marglin 1998).

Clarkson, Morrissette, and Regallet (1992) characterise the main divergence in conceptions of ecological knowledge as sacred (indigenous) and secular (Western) perspectives (13). The dominant secular perspective views ecosystems as passive entities that consist of resources that can be endlessly exploited to satisfy human needs (1992, 12). Human thoughts, emotions, and actions are compartmentalised, deemed to exist on a plane separate from the earth's natural ecosystems. This contrasts with a sacred perspective, which aims to balance the needs of the community with the needs of the individual and the earth. In this relational view, humans do not control natural ecosystems but rather live in a sustainable, harmonious relationship with them (1992, 10). David Suzuki (1997) refers to this as a sacred balance between humans and the natural world that has existed since time immemorial. He stresses that humans depend upon natural ecologies for survival, that they are central to our essence, and that it is only very recently, in the long span of human life, that we began to think otherwise (15–16). This shift, not only in how humans think but also in how we impact our environment, concurs with what is beginning to be recognised as a new geological epoch: the *Anthropocene*, in which human activities have a significant global impact on the world's ecosystems (Boykoff and Yulsman 2013, 359), and in the end risk destroying them. Urry (2011) notes that in Western Europe and North America the late 19th century, when nature was *irreversibly transformed* (which signifies the beginning of this transcendence into the *Anthropocene*), was also the period when this unfortunate epistemological division between nature and society reached its climax. The same period was also marked by a huge increase in dissemination and visualisation in the media sector, as well as the peak of imperialism with its condescending view of 'other' people (Roosvall, 2016).

In a counter-hegemonic move, researchers, policy makers, and activists alike have recently begun to acknowledge that indigenous knowledge can play an important role in understanding and helping to mitigate climate change (Hulme 2009, 81–82; Huntington 2013; Tipa 2009; Tauli-Corpuz et al. 2009). Deborah McGregor observes several cases where TEK has already started to play a role in sustainable development initiatives (McGregor 2002, 2004). However, she notes that key differences in how indigenous and non-indigenous peoples relate to TEK have posed challenges for conservation initiatives that draw insights from both worldviews (see also Tipa 2009). Indigenous peoples with their long tradition of adapting to climate change could lead the way in adaptation initiatives (Tauli-Corpuz et al. 2009), if these challenges are resolved.

Defining Media Ecology

Media ecology and 'ecology of communication' are both concepts used to refer to media and communication as an environment. 'Ecology of communication' details how information and communication technologies operate and are intertwined with activity (Altheide 1994). Media ecology refers more particularly to the study of media as environments. Both conceptualisations resonate with the general definition of ecology as the relationship between a group of living things and their environment (see Introduction). In this chapter we use the term media ecology in order to underline our interest in studying representations of Traditional Ecological Knowledge in *mediated* communication, both in terms of its outcomes and its conditions.

Media ecologists study interactions between humans and mediated communication in a range of different historical and cultural contexts (McLuhan 1964; Nystrom 1973; Postman 1985). According to Neil Postman, the words 'media' and 'ecology' are combined in order to:

> [...] make people more conscious of the fact that human beings live in two different kinds of environments. One is the natural environment and consists of things like air, trees, rivers, and caterpillars. The other is the media environment, which consists of language, numbers, images, holograms, and all of the other symbols, techniques, and machinery that make us what we are (Postman 2000, 11)

Like natural environments, the ways in which humans interface with media have profound effects on our thoughts, feelings, and actions (ibid.) in what Mark Deuze (2012) calls 'media life'. Consequently, media ecologists study these influences by focusing on the structure, content, and impact of a media environment, rather than by isolating one of these factors while neglecting others (Logan 2007, 21). This ecological approach to studying media resonates with TEK's holistic conception of the relation between knowledge and life. We explore this resemblance here by discussing indigenous activists' views on the media ecologies that affect their lives and consider how this relates to their views on natural ecology.

Building on this theoretical foundation, Robert Logan (2007) calls for studies that bridge biological nature and media environments. He does this in order to establish that media function as 'living organisms'. This extends the scope of media ecology beyond the study of interactions between media to encompassing biological nature (2007, 21). In line with TEK, Logan contends that it is not adequate to study biology and culture separately since '[...] human evolution is a combination of biological and cultural evolution' (2007, 21). Just as natural ecosystems must be studied relationally as 'emergent phenomena', so too must media ecologists turn their attention toward biology and the nonlinear dynamics that influence media systems. Here the key point is that one cannot possibly isolate certain elements of media or natural ecosystems and study them independently.

Christine Tracy uses these theoretical insights to explain why the prevailing 'ecology of news' consistently fails to challenge the existing beliefs of media consumers and producers (2012, 134–135). This occurs in spite of the sophistication of contemporary information and communication technology. It has become increasingly challenging to process the tremendous volume of news and information circulated by news media. Tracy explains that as '[...] the amount of information provided increases, its significance and value decreases' (2012, 136). The consequence is 'perceptual bias', a symptom of news overload that causes audiences to only process information that reinforces what they already know. This, as we shall see, poses significant challenges for those concerned with raising awareness of alternative perspectives on environmental issues.

The 'perceptual bias' Tracy identifies as a limitation of the prevailing news ecology resonates with the challenges indigenous activists face in trying to get their message across in mainstream media (Roosvall and Tegelberg 2015). In other words, it may be because TEK represents a different worldview that it seldom occupies a central position in the news ecology. Media produced by indigenous activists have however been concluded to be capable of countering prevailing myths and assumptions (Avison and Meadows 2000; Alia 2001; Russell 2005; Pietikäinen 2008; Hafsteinsson and Bredin 2010). A primary aim of indigenous produced media is to resonate more closely with the identities and lived experiences of indigenous peoples. In this chapter, we are not interested in continuing to lament the fact that indigenous peoples are ignored by mainstream media. Instead our focus is on calls made and steps taken *by* indigenous actors to reform coverage of climate change in the news media ecosystem.

Method and Material

This study focuses on interviews conducted with indigenous activists at COP17 in Durban, South Africa in December 2011.[2] During the summit we conducted six interviews with activists from indigenous organisations representing natural ecosystems from across the globe. One interview included two interviewees. The interviewees were:

- Curtis Konek and Jordan Konek of the Inuit Youth Delegation, Arviat, Nunavut, Canada;

- Vibeke Larsen, a Sámi politician from Norway;

- Raymond de Chavez of Tebtebba, an umbrella organisation representing a network of indigenous groups;

- Tito Puanchir, President of the Confederation of Indigenous Nationalities of the Ecuadorian Amazon (CONFENIAE);

- Tiina Kurvits of Many Strong Voices, an advocacy organisation that promotes security and sustainability in coastal communities in the Arctic and in small island developing states;

- François Paulette, former Chief of Smith's Landing First Nation, Northwest Territories, Canada

Some of these organisations are associated with a particular ecosystem: the Inuit Youth Delegation with the Arctic ecosystem and CONFENIAE with 'tropical and sub-tropical ecosystems'. Others have a mandate that

---

2   The same interviews are referred to in an article on media geographies of climate justice (Roosvall and Tegelberg 2015). The focus here, however, is different. We highlight ecological aspects of media and nature and how these may intersect, rather than focusing on how aspects of justice are intertwined with geographical scales. We chose the umbrella term 'indigenous activists' to refer to the interviewees. However, differences within the group make them connect to this term to varying degrees. While she is not of indigenous descent, Tina Kurvits works for an organisation advocating for justice for Arctic communities and small island states, which are mostly constituted by indigenous peoples. Vibeke Larsen, in turn, is a politician with the Sami parliament that works within the Norwegian delegation. All interviewees are united by their advocacy for indigenous rights in relation to climate change.

encompasses several ecosystems: Many Strong Voices covers the Arctic as well as 'coastal and marine ecosystems' and Tebtebba speaks to the range of different ecosystems inhabited by the indigenous groups this organisation represents. Sámi and First Nations representatives, Vibeke Larsen and François Paulette, account for large national territories with several ecosystems. In Vibeke Larsen's case, the Arctic is significant because of the Sámi's representation on the Arctic council. Climate change continues to have severe impacts across the northern regions of the Nordic countries and parts of Western Russia, which together constitute the traditional Sámi territories (Sápmi). Climate and ecosystems are mixed in Norway. Part of Norway is situated within an Arctic (tundra) climate, part in a subarctic climate and a boreal ecosystem, etc. Similarly, François Paulette's community lies in Canada's vast northern boreal forest ecosystem, one of the world's largest carbon basins.

The interviews took place either outside the official summit halls in an NGO tent or at the main entrance where some of the activists were demonstrating. We posed four basic questions about climate change, media reporting, and indigenous peoples:

- What do you think about media coverage of indigenous peoples and climate change?

- Is there a difference between mainstream media and alternative media reporting on indigenous peoples and climate change?

- Do you have an opinion on how media coverage could be improved?

- Do you have advice for media researchers on how to approach these issues in future research?

We focus here on the first three questions (for elaboration on question 4, please see Roosvall and Tegelberg 2015), taking Alan Bryman's (1996, 46) position that open-ended interviews help to facilitate analysis of social matters from the perspectives of the actors involved. In accordance with this emphasis on the perspectives of interviewees, we use extensive quotes from our open-ended interviews to ensure that the voices of our respondents are heard.

Our interview analysis draws on critical discourse analysis in order to describe structures of texts (in this case transcribed talk) and relate them to social, political, and cultural contexts (see van Dijk 2000). We focus on what can be termed key themes or topics (Berglez 2008; van Dijk 1988, 2000).[3] These are distinguished with the help of our theoretical approach and categorised accordingly into two groups of statements: one relating to natural ecology and the other relating to media ecology. The themes are subsequently discussed with attention to power relations. In particular, power relations concerning diverging views on ecology (for instance TEK vs. Western knowledge) and power relations between indigenous people and the media. In distinguishing themes, Olausson (2009, 424) asks 'which themes and topics — e.g., statements, discussions, questions, arguments — are granted prominence (in a hierarchical order)' (see also Berglez 2008; van Dijk 1988). We apply this approach to the interviewees' responses to our questions, and focus on *how* themes and topics (statements, discussions, questions, arguments) are granted prominence, within the frames of the theoretically determined themes, media ecology vs. natural ecology, and how subthemes are related to these frames.

The discussion of results follows the thematic methodological approach and is thereby divided into two main parts. The first focuses on statements concerning the natural ecosystems threatened by climate change and steps taken by indigenous peoples to defend these threatened territories. The second part concerns statements regarding the news media ecology and its limitations.

The interview analysis is combined with analysis of materials collected through basic participant observation (Iorio 2011) at the summit. In this chapter we will evoke those parts of our participatory observation that included collection of material and documentation of the communicative environment of the interviewees, mainly focusing on

---

3   In Berglez's (2008) and van Dijk's (1988) accounts, thematic analysis is merely one part of critical discourse analysis. It is generally combined with schematic analysis, micro-analysis of texts, and analysis of the sociocultural context. Because schematic analysis is suited to manufactured texts, particularly media texts, rather than utterances in interviews, it is not considered here (although we do of course pay attention to utterances that are emphasized by interviewees). We connect loosely to the microanalysis of texts by paying attention to power relations. However, the bulk of our emphasis is at the thematic level, where we distinguish how natural and media ecology themes are constructed by interviewees. The sociocultural context is addressed in the contextualization of our results.

their booths in the NGO tent.[4] Photographs can be used as part of visual methodology, for instance in the form of photo documentation (Rose 2011). We have used a basic form of this here, documenting how the activists themselves communicate through material displayed in their booths as well as how they present themselves in official performances. We use some of this material to contextualise and add to the interview material.

Analysis

Talking about Traditional Ecological Knowledge

In interviews with indigenous activists from areas with diverging natural ecologies, we observed a pattern of recognising a balance, sometimes framed as a sacred balance, with the natural environment that has endured for generations. Each interviewee alludes to the importance of maintaining a holistic relationship with a particular natural ecosystem; that is, they allude to central features of Traditional Ecological Knowledge.

Without naming it explicitly, Tito Puanchir (*CONFENIAE*) explains how TEK informs relations between Amazonian indigenous peoples and the natural world.[5] Puanchir says:

> [...] we live in the Amazon jungle and we have territories where there is lots of biodiversity with natural resources like water and air. We have an intimate relation with nature, with all living things. This is the reason why we care for the environment, why we give back with benevolence instead of destroying it, which we do not think is a good approach. How one manages the environment depends on how one understands it.

There is no separation between nature, culture, and spirituality in this Amazonian worldview. Local decisions about how to use the land stem from this holistic understanding. Puanchir proceeds to elaborate on the ways in which this intimate relationship with the natural world informs

---

4   Our previous research (Roosvall and Tegelberg 2015) elaborates on the experience of taking part in press events organised by these organisations.
5   The interview with Puanchir was originally conducted in Spanish and later translated into English by Matthew Tegelberg.

community decisions regarding the management and conservation of resources:

> I believe our ancestors foresaw what was going to happen. They performed a ritual in front of the waterfall; a place where they went to find strength, to better understand the world, what is happening and what will come to pass in the future. They used that knowledge, as well, to manage existing resources [...] for us, the waterfall is sacred [...] our god rests in that place and protects the jungle. If we intervene massively, if we chop down the trees and contaminate the water, all of these things and all these beings will disappear [...] we will be left with nothing.

In this worldview, resource management processes are informed by consultation with the natural world itself. Rupturing this sacred balance between humans and the local ecology places the health and spiritual well-being of the Amazonian community at risk.

The essence of Puanchir's statements corresponds to what Guttorm (2011) underlines as the feature that distinguishes Sámi views on TEK from other local perspectives; namely that it includes a spiritual dimension. This view is reminiscent of the Andean worldview detailed by Frederique Apffel-Marglin (1998). Indigenous approaches to human-nature relationships thus seem to transcend ecosystems, as the Sámi mainly connect to the Arctic, Puanchir to the tropical/subtropical ecology, and Andean views to high altitude and high montane ecosystems.

When asked how to raise better awareness of the climate challenges Amazonian indigenous peoples must confront, Puanchir places emphasis on intergenerational education that integrates TEK:

> We are also working on a bilingual, intercultural Amazonian educational curriculum which we want to transform into a formal education system to help children learn how to protect and care for the jungle. This is for children from birth and for new parents who must encourage children to know and develop a relationship with nature from birth through their academic formation.

Taken together these statements attest to the importance of TEK for past, present, and future generations. The past is evoked through a focus on ancestors and ancient spiritual rituals; the present through statements on deforestation and contemporary strategies to stop such practices; and, the future, in Puanchir's emphasis on planning new curricula that help children and new parents become conscious of the importance of preserving a sacred balance with nature.

Fig. 4.1 Inuit Youth Delegation Booth in the NGO tent

This bridging of past, present, and future was mirrored at the Inuit Youth Delegation's booth in the NGO tent (Figure 4.1). A storyboard containing a series of picture panels draws attention to ongoing changes in the relations between Inuit and the Arctic ecosystem. The first panel, labelled 'past', depicts community members practicing TEK. Pictures associated with the *past* feature two hunters cleaning a caribou, a dog team traveling across the frozen Arctic tundra, and other images depicting traditional foods. Pictures of the *present* depict change as well as continuity with the past. Change is represented by a picture of young people crowded around a computer and another of a supermarket aisle lined with boxes of Kraft dinner. The adjacent images show continuity with the past, connecting present and past in accordance with TEK: we see a young man at work cleaning a caribou, and an elder showcasing her handicrafts. Pictures from past and present stand in sharp contrast to the empty panels under the label 'future'. The blank panels attest to the uncertainty that surrounds TEK's future role in the Arctic ecosystem due to the impacts of climate change. Rapid changes in the Arctic ecosystem are eroding the balanced relation between Inuit and their natural surroundings. Risks to the natural ecosystem, in other words, are directly correlated with community health risks.

Our interview with Curtis Konek of the Inuit Youth Organization underlines the conflict between TEK and Western science and stresses that aspects of TEK are not granted sufficient attention (see also Roosvall and Tegelberg 2015). Vibeke Larsen, a Sámi Representative with the Norwegian Delegation, alludes to a conflict between TEK and Western science in a similar way. Larsen comments on the impact renewable energy projects are having on the traditional reindeer herding territories they encroach upon in northern Norway. She says:

> [...] they have to take some reindeer inland to build this [windmills] and you have to build roads into it and all the wires. So you have to take a lot of land. Then they come into conflict with the Sámi reindeer herding and you are in conflict between climate and the traditional way to live. So that's where the Sámi parliament comes in [...] we consult with the Norwegian society, how can we do this without too much influence on the reindeer herding but still have the green energy because it [*sic*] will benefit, we will benefit in the long term from green energy. So it's a hard place for the Sámi parliament because we want to be responsible for society, we want to be responsible for our future, and, at the same time, we have to take care of our old culture and the reindeer herding. (See also Roosvall and Tegelberg 2015)

Here Larsen identifies conflicts that can arise between two different climate-friendly initiatives: the former linked to Western scientific strategies for adaptation and mitigation (a national wind energy project); and the latter rooted in TEK (traditional reindeer herding) (see also Roosvall and Tegelberg 2015). The statement underscores that even development initiatives widely viewed as climate-friendly may create conditions that pose added threats to locally practiced TEK. A holistic view helps underline that all of these 'side-effects', and how they in turn may disturb ecosystems, need to be taken into consideration.

Raymond de Chavez of Tebtebba says:

> [...] indigenous peoples have really managed and conserved forests through generations, so when you talk of REDD indigenous peoples should be central to the whole discussion. And so we are [trying] to ensure that indigenous concerns are included in the REDD architecture.

REDD, a UN programme, is short for Reduced Emissions from Deforestation and Forest Degradation. When combined with the new REDD+ initiative, a climate change mitigation solution, this programme includes the issues of deforestation and forest degradation as well as the role of conservation, enhancement of forest carbon stocks and sustainable forest management.[6] Raymond de Chavez stresses that indigenous peoples' TEK perspective on the management and conservation of forests means they should be at the centre of REDD policy discussions. Yet, as de Chavez implies, this knowledge is rarely considered. Similar conflicts have been noted in the Australian context where Aboriginal and conservation interests have been polarised (Adams 2004). Michael Adams (2004) notes, however, that collaborations can bridge these gaps while at the same time bridging gaps between non-indigenous and indigenous peoples more generally.

François Paulette identifies an economic aspect of ecological conflicts by describing how national economic interests in Canada threaten the boreal ecosystem: '[...] they [the Canadian government] are increasing the tar sands output which will destroy more environment [...] the river, the people'. Paulette invokes TEK to suggest that Canadians should become more ecologically conscious. He urges Canadians to '[...] have more of a conscience, not a political conscience but more of an environmental conscience, more of a *spiritual* conscience about the land, the earth and us human beings' (emphasis added). Tina Kurvits of Many Strong Voices echoes the point that the scope of TEK does not have to be limited to indigenous peoples. For example, she explains that '[...] in Newfoundland, there are no indigenous people [...] but the Newfoundlanders have been there for centuries so local knowledge

---

6   See http://www.un-redd.org/AboutREDD/tabid/102614/Default.aspx, see also Eide 2012, 87.

is really important. If you've been there for three, four hundred years you know something more than a government scientist coming in for the first time'. Kurvits points to local knowledge as part of TEK, which corresponds with Guttorm's (2011) aforementioned approximation of indigenous and local knowledge. The exception being that local knowledge, in Guttorm's view, does not include a spiritual angle on the holistic human-nature relation.

Indigenous Perspectives on Media Ecologies

While none of the interviewees make explicit references to media ecology in their comments on media coverage, many stress that what we term the news media ecology should be enhanced to raise greater awareness of ecological issues. Interviewees speak of the limitations of a national news ecology dominated by mainstream media, which reinforces the status quo and rarely makes room for indigenous perspectives or knowledge of climate change. They also comment on the ways in which their own media practices, situated within diverse news ecologies, attempt to create dialogue and generate awareness of these issues.

When asked about coverage of indigenous perspectives on climate change, Tina Kurvits of Many Strong Voices, the organisation focused on Arctic communities as well as small island states, stresses that: '[...] in the mainstream media we're not seeing an awful lot [...] once in a while there might be something but it tends to focus on say the polar bears, as opposed to the impact on the people that would be hunting bears or that are dependent on the wildlife on the land. So overall [...] I'm certainly not overwhelmed by it [the coverage]'. When indigenous perspectives are featured in climate stories, Kurvits suggests they fall under two categories. The story is either sensational, and therefore picked up by mainstream media for its dramatic appeal, or the scope of the coverage is limited to local or regional news media.

Regarding the attention that *does* occur in some instances Kurvits says: '[...] it tends to be when there is a dramatic event, it's not really about making connections to what climate means to people living in these regions that are immediately affected by it and that are really dependent on their immediate environment'. She adds later that: '[...]

when you see things being covered [in Canada] it would be more in say the northern papers, or in the papers from the regions'. Kurvits implies here that it is national rather than local or regional coverage that is ideal. This, as we shall soon see, is something several interviewees indicate without making it explicit.

Kurvits is also critical of the news media's failure to make the connection between climate change and the livelihoods of the indigenous peoples it affects. She goes on to explain that this shortcoming was the catalyst for 'Portraits of Resilience' (http://www.manystrongvoices. org/portraits/), a campaign that has generated some media attention. However, she notes that these events tend to draw more attention from alternative and local media than they do from mainstream outlets. Kurvits' organisation Many Strong Voices features a celebrity endorsement (from Richard Branson) as a banner that appears above all its webpages. This reinforces points Kurvits makes in the interview about having to stage sensational media events (the example she gives is bringing together iconic indigenous and island state leaders in the same place) in order to get the mainstream media to pay any attention to the issues.

Alison Anderson (2013) notes that the practice of using celebrities to capture media attention for, in this case, climate change in the Arctic, can be very effective. Yet, at the same time, the intended message can become altered or even disappear. This coincides with our own findings from studies of media reporting on indigenous peoples and climate change (Roosvall and Tegelberg 2012, 2013): indigenous activists seem to get the most attention if they stand out by wearing traditional clothing, but this focus on cultural identity tends, at the same time, to either alter the political messages they try to deliver or make them disappear. The media focus on the clothing is parallel to the sensationalism in this sense. Our basic participant observations showed that many indigenous activists wear traditional clothing (wholly or partly) at public events like demonstrations and press gatherings, as well as when they tend to their booths in the NGO area. As we have mentioned elsewhere (Roosvall and Tegelberg 2015), the Inuit Youth Delegation quickly changed into traditional clothing after arriving late for a press event (due to a traffic jam) wearing jeans and sneakers.

Fig. 4.2 Press event with the Inuit Youth Delegation in the NGO tent

Fig. 4.3 Tito Puanchir of the Confederation of Indigenous Nationalities of the Ecuadorian Amazon being interviewed by Matthew Tegelberg in the NGO tent

The purpose of mentioning the connection between the media's focus on traditional clothing and the simultaneous downplaying of politics that is often noticeable in articles is not meant to indicate that indigenous peoples should not wear traditional clothing in order to have their political messages respected, but rather to identify what seems like a pattern in media reporting. It is this pattern of media representations, rather than indigenous self-representations, which must be scrutinised.

Like Kurvits, above, several other activists reiterate the negligence of mainstream national media in reporting indigenous perspectives on climate change. At the same time, the consensus is that it is mainstream and national media attention that these indigenous activists seek. Jordan Konek of the Inuit Youth Delegation discusses the importance of the CBC, the national Canadian broadcaster, and its lack of coverage of indigenous issues/perspectives:

> CBC National should be around here because they are [...] known for really getting the idea out. I mean they are pretty much the deal, if they wanna spread something they'll spread it and the Canadians will find out what's going on [...] I think that CBC News — The National [the flagship news program] should have been here, or they should be here, filming these kind of things because we are the people that are experiencing the problems and they should spread it.

Jordan Konek underlines the importance of the mainstream national media. He proceeds to elaborate further, explaining that:

> [...] the best way to improve media is to share, share what's most important. If media, let's say CBC and CTV [Canada's largest privately owned TV network] shared [...] because this [climate change] is a serious issue [...] that is gonna affect our lives in the future and if they share it together instead of competing against each other I think that would be the best way to improve their media skills, only they'll do what they like.

Jordan Konek echoes the concerns raised by Kurvits about the lack of attention mainstream Canadian media pay to the Inuit people affected by climate change. CBC News — The National is a nightly news broadcast that Konek identifies as the primary agenda setter in the Canadian news media ecology. He concludes that national mainstream media, like the CBC and CTV, need to relate to each other in new ways; that is, they need to stop competing and start sharing. Without this collaboration it is unlikely Canadians will be informed of the local challenges Inuit are facing in the Arctic. The statement criticises the established media ecology and calls for a new, differently balanced one.

After criticising Canada's mainstream media for failing to generate awareness of Arctic climate change, Jordan and Curtis Konek discuss their own strategies of communicating via social media.

> Curtis Konek: We blog when we feel like blogging and we blog when we hear something interesting from an elder [...].
> Jordan Konek: A lot of the films that I've put together are on the Nanisiniq website (http://nanisiniq.tumblr.com/), where we post [...] the views that we're getting are pretty good and the blogs we're gonna be posting a lot more of it. And I'm gonna be putting a blog sometime this week talking about what I think about coming here and to see how I feel about seeing other walks of life cause this is completely different from my culture, so yeah, we're gonna be sharing lots about Durban.

They emphasise the importance of 'sharing knowledge', explaining how community members have begun using social media platforms (YouTube, Tumblr, Twitter) to document and share indigenous knowledge of climate change.

François Paulette suggests that efforts to raise awareness of indigenous issues in mainstream media are futile since they represent the interests of corporate stakeholders. He says that the 'Mainstream media are conservative [...] It [*sic*] supports the views of right-wing leaders, sides with industry [...] most of the papers in the world are right wing conservative papers so they reflect the profile of industry and governments rather that the people'. Paulette thus underscores the political leanings of most mainstream media outlets and highlights their connection to corporations and governments. His statements scrutinise the same mainstream media from which most interviewees want attention. He problematises the ecology of the national news media system further as he talks about indigenous media on the *national* level, when he mentions *Aboriginal Peoples Television Network* (APTN) as an alternative to dominant mainstream narratives about climate change and its effects on indigenous peoples. The national media ecology does in fact encompass indigenous programming and channels in some countries like Canada (and Sweden, Norway, etc.), but this is seldom taken into consideration when the national media ecology is discussed.

Larsen echoes Paulette's critique of mainstream media coverage: 'The mainstream media in Norway don't cover indigenous problems anyway. So they cover climate changes but they don't cover the indigenous aspect in the climate change'. The mainstream media ignore particular experiences of climate change in northern indigenous communities that are marginalised in Norwegian media generally. Larsen stresses that one of the key problems is that large, corporate media do not know anything about indigenous peoples and that they should make more of an effort to get to know indigenous peoples and understand their perspectives. Larsen does not address the issue of alternative media much, aside from noting that there are two main types of Sámi media: Sámi radio and print media. It is interesting that these come up as alternative media, where alternative is likely understood as an alternative to non-indigenous media. Such non-indigenous media is media that indigenous groups must relate to. As our interviews show, indigenous activists try to balance the bias of non-indigenous media by offering other perspectives, either from within or outside these media.

One way of offering other perspectives is to become the media, much like the strategies the Koneks discuss above. Raymond de Chavez from Tebtebba mentions having a Twitter account and using digital social media (Twitter and Facebook) to get the message out. He also discusses how the organisation uses email and social media platforms to stay in touch. These communication technologies are essential for transnational organisations, like Tebtebba, that do not have the bankroll to bring together widely dispersed group members. While becoming the media is a strategy for many activists, and one that often takes place in the realm of digital social media within the wider media ecology, the importance of legacy media is consistently underlined in parallel with these online and social media practices.

Tito Puanchir talks further about the importance of raising consciousness among local Amazonian communities by using not only digital, but also local, legacy media to disseminate information:

> [...] in the first place information is power [...] we have, through the national government, started to work with communities toward implementing Internet and telephones and we want this to eventually cover all the communities of the Amazon. Another strategy is to widen the scope of coverage on indigenous radio, so they can broadcast on what

is happening in the communities in their own languages [...] [At] the universities [...] we want to create virtual classrooms so that information can be known throughout the country. For example in places that are difficult to access, we need to cooperate with the universities but we don't have the resources to do this on our own.

Puanchir relates to multiple geographical levels when he talks about the media ecology. The national is important since governments need to be involved, and so are the local communities where radio can be broadcast in local languages. Puanchir thus brings up a crucial feature of the media ecologies: language. This is something that could be added to the divisions we made initially: to mainstream vs. alternative, national vs. local, and non-indigenous vs. indigenous media, and the different ways in which they intersect. Thus we add national language (and 'global English' media) vs. local indigenous language media and consider how this distinction intersects with the others. Distinctions are also made by the interviewees between social media and mainstream media, as mentioned in the examples of media strategies applied by de Chavez and the Koneks. When asked about possible differences between mainstream and alternative media, several interviewees associated alternative media with social media (see also Roosvall and Tegelberg 2015). While these media were seen as significant for representing the voices of indigenous peoples, they were not seen as sufficient for bringing the messages to wider audiences.

Conclusions

This chapter has detailed how natural and media ecosystems are (dis) connected in mediated communication on climate change. Across the interviews, a number of subthemes emerge in statements interviewees make about the ecology of news and how it relates to views on natural ecology, particularly their own views on Traditional Ecological Knowledge. These subthemes can be identified: the crucial role of national mainstream media; the crucial role of indigenous media (these roles are inherently different yet connected to each other); and a perceived conflict between TEK and Western views and practices. The most common subtheme, 'the crucial role of national mainstream media', includes the contention that national mainstream media fail to adequately represent indigenous perspectives. This concern is identified, at least implicitly, by each of the indigenous activists we interviewed. Vibeke Larsen implies that the mainstream media are not even aware of what indigenous perspectives encompass. Others, like François Paulette, contend that ignoring these perspectives is politically and economically motivated. Hence media logic in the mainstream realm of the news ecology is strongly connected to power. In the prevailing media ecology, it is necessary to connect to this power if a message is to be widely heard and respected. Consequently, it makes sense that all the actors share the consensus that getting indigenous voices and views into the mainstream media is crucial for raising awareness of the issues they face. Some interviewees, however, point to the need for a re-balancing of current media ecologies — which unlike natural ecologies are constructed ecologies closely connected to distribution of means — as some of the traits of the second subtheme, 'the crucial role of indigenous media', reveals.

Regarding 'the crucial role of indigenous media', many interviewees refer to examples of indigenous-produced media designed to respond to a lack of interest in indigenous views in mainstream media. The significance of this subtheme in the interview material can be summed up as follows: firstly, it demonstrates the limitations of mainstream media coverage of climate change, which mostly ignores indigenous perspectives and experiences in addition to content produced by indigenous media. Secondly, it points to an imbalance in prevailing news media ecologies that justifies calls for reform or even a complete restructuring with new boundaries: changes that make room for these neglected perspectives to be articulated more widely. Finally, among interviewees, alternative media seems to mean producing your own content on digital social media platforms; indigenous actors turn to these platforms (examples given include Twitter, YouTube, blogs, and Tumblr) to disseminate their own messages.

However, most interviewees do not seem confident that the message has a wide enough impact when limited to alternative and social media channels. Hence the questions that remain are: To what extent is the general public exposed to media produced by indigenous actors? Should indigenous peoples be solely responsible for their own media coverage? What adaptations can be made to mainstream media ecologies to help indigenous activists bringing their stories to the public? Or conversely, and more importantly, how can mainstream media adapt to the urgency of climate change by giving a voice to indigenous activists and their perspectives on natural ecologies?

The third subtheme concerning 'a perceived conflict between TEK and Western views/practices' is strongly connected to the first two subthemes. There is an urge to share indigenous perspectives, and especially TEK approaches, with the rest of the world in order to save the planet at the global and the local (their own communities or territories) scale. In order to share these perspectives, mainstream media are still deemed necessary. Similarly, local or national indigenous media are considered the channels where these perspectives *can* be shared. However, as previously noted, this media is often produced in indigenous languages. This is important *per se* but, at the same time, limits the scope of this coverage to local audiences (except for the few nation-states where indigenous groups are dominant). Hence the perceived conflict between diverging perspectives on nature and ecology, particularly concerning the human-nature relationship and conservation, is mirrored in a conflict between mainstream national and indigenous local media. Thus, we can conclude that these subthemes create connections between the main media ecology theme and the natural ecology theme, indicating that they are intertwined through the particular disconnection of TEK views on natural ecology from the mainstream national non-indigenous news ecology, whether this is expressed in analogue or digital platforms.

Mike Hulme (2009) notes that climate change is not only an environmental but also a cultural and political phenomenon. It is reshaping the ways we understand ourselves as human beings and our place in the world, much as the 'media life' we live (Deuze 2012) and the media ecologies that surround us help shape our thoughts. In a world threatened by climate change, there is a balance in natural ecologies that *must not* be disturbed (but has already been disturbed), while there is an imbalance in media ecologies that *must* be disturbed so that it becomes more inclusive of indigenous voices and traditional ecological knowledge on a level that reaches large audiences. Our results indicate the potential for reshaping dominant perceptions of climate change through reshaping media ecologies bounded by nation-states. To achieve this these ecologies must be more inclusive of indigenous voices and perspectives and less focused on the nation-state level as a naturalised level of understanding climate change. In addition, they must move beyond the nation-state hegemony's connections to modernity, which downplay holistic views on human-nature relationships. Such developments can, in turn, play a positive role in preserving the natural ecologies that are currently threatened by climate change. By marginalising indigenous perspectives on climate change, journalists have missed an opportunity to gain valuable insights and foster critical dialogue between communities with divergent views on how to respond to climate change. If one thing is certain, despite differences in the national media ecologies and natural ecologies that these indigenous activists relate to, the interviewees each offer similar takes on the complete disconnect between their own views on natural ecology and those represented in prevailing media ecologies.

References

Adams, Michael, 'Negotiating Nature: Collaboration and Conflict Between Aboriginal and Conservation Interests in New South Wales, Australia', *Australian Journal of Environmental Education*, 20(1) (2004), 3–12.

Alia, Valerie, *Un/Covering the North: News, Media and Aboriginal People* (Vancouver: University of British Columbia Press, 2001).

Altheide, David L., 'An Ecology of Communication: Toward a Mapping of the Effective Environment', *The Sociology Quarterly*, 35(4) (1994), 665–683, http://dx.doi.org/10.1111/j.1533-8525.1994.tb00422.x

Anaya, James, 'Report of the Special Rapporteur on the Situation of Human Rights and Fundamental Freedoms of Indigenous People. Addendum: The Situation of the Sami People in the Sápmi Region of Norway, Sweden and Finland'. Human Rights Council, 18th Session, Agenda Item 3, 12 January 2011, www.samer.se/3543

Anderson, Alison, '"Together We Can Save the Arctic": Celebrity Advocacy and the Rio Earth Summit 2012', *Celebrity Studies*, 4(3) (2013), 339–352, http://dx.doi.org/10.1080/19392397.2013.831617

Anderson, Mark C. and Robertson, Carmen L., *Seeing Red: A History of Natives in Canadian Newspapers* (Winnipeg: University of Manitoba Press, 2011).

Apffel-Marglin, Frederique, *The Spirit of Regeneration: Andean Culture Confronting Western Notions of Development* (London: Zed Books, 1998).

Atton, Chris, *Alternative Media* (London: Sage Publications, 2002).

Avison, Shannon and Meadows, Michael, 'Speaking and Hearing: Aboriginal Newspapers and the Public Sphere in Canada and Australia', *Canadian Journal of Communication*, 25(3) (2000), 347–366.

Berglez, Peter, 'Kritisk diskursanalys', in *Metoder ikommunikationsvetenskap*, ed. by Mats Ekström and Larsake Larsson (Lund: Studentlitteratur, 2008).

Boykoff, Maxwell, T., and Yulsman, Tom, 'Political Economy, Media and Climate Change: Sinews of Modern Life', *WIREs Climate Change*, 4(5) (2013), 359–371, http://dx.doi.org/10.1002/wcc.233

Bryman, Alan, *Social Research Methods* (Oxford: Oxford University Press, 1996).

Clarkson, Linda, Morrissette, Vern and Regallet, Gabriel, *Our Responsibility to the Seventh Generation: Indigenous Peoples and Sustainable Development* (Winnipeg: International Institute for Sustainable Development, 1992).

Deuze, Mark, *Media Life* (Cambridge: Polity, 2012).

Eide, Elisabeth, 'Saving the Rain Forest — Differing Perspectives. Norways Climate and Forest Initiative and Reporting in Three Countries', in *Media Meets Climate: The Global Challenge for Journalism*, ed. by Elisabeth Eide and Risto Kunelius (Gotheburg: Nordicom, 2012), pp. 87–104.

Eriksen, Christine and Adams, Michael, 'Indigenous Environmental Knowledge', in *Encyclopedia of Geography*, ed. by Barney Warf (London: Sage, 2010), pp. 1–3.

Guttorm, Gunvor, 'Árbediehtu (Sami Traditional Knowledge) as a Concept and in Practice', in *Working with Traditional Knowledge: Communities, Institutions, Information Systems, Law and Ethics*, ed. by Jelena Porsanger and Gunvor Guttorm (Kautokeino: Norway Sámi allaskuvla), pp. 59–76.

Hafsteinsson, Sigurjón Baldur, and Bredin, Marian, *Indigenous Screen Cultures in Canada* (Winnipeg: University of Manitoba Press, 2010).

Harcup, Tony, '"The Unspoken — Said": The Journalism of Alternative Media', *Journalism*, 4(3) (2003), 356–376, http://dx.doi.org/10.1177/14648849030043006

Hulme, Mike, *Why We Disagree About Climate Change* (Cambridge: Cambridge University Press, 2009), http://dx.doi.org/10.1017/cbo9780511841200

Huntington, Henry, 'A Question of Scale: Local versus Pan-Arctic Impacts from Sea-Ice Change', in *Media and the Politics of Arctic Climate Change: When the Ice Breaks*, ed. by Miyase Christensen, Annika E. Nilsson and Nina Wormbs (Basingstoke: Palgrave Macmillan, 2013), pp. 114–127, http://dx.doi.org/10.1057/9781137266231_6

Iorio, Sharon Hartin, *Research in Journalism: Taking it to the Streets* (London: Routledge, 2011).

Knudsen, Susanne, 'Intersectionality — A Theoretical Inspiration in the Analysis of Minority Cultures and Identities in Textbooks', in *Eighth International Conference on Learning and Educational Media: Caught in the Web or Lost in the Textbook?*, ed. by Éric Bruillard, Bente Aamotsbakken, Susanne Knudsen and Mike Horsley (Normandie, Paris: Jouve, 2006), pp. 61–76, https://iartemblog.files.wordpress.com/2012/03/8th_iartem_2005-conference.pdf

Logan, Robert K., 'The Biological Foundation of Media Ecology', *Explorations in Media Ecology*, 6(1) (2007), 19–34.

McGregor, Deborah, 'Coming Full Circle: Indigenous Knowledge, Environment, and Our Future', *American Indian Quarterly*, 28(3–4) (2004), 385–410.

—, 'Traditional Ecological Knowledge and the Two-Row Wampum', *Biodiversity*, 3(3) (2002), pp. 8–9, http://dx.doi.org/10.1080/14888386.2002.9712586

McLuhan, Marshall, *Understanding Media: The Extensions of Man* (New York: McGraw-Hill, 1964).

Merriam-Webster Online, 'Ecology', [n.date], http://www.merriam-webster.com/dictionary/ecology

Nystrom, Christine, *Towards a Science of Media Ecology: The Formulation of Integrated Conceptual Paradigms for the Study of Human Communication Systems* (Doctoral thesis, New York University, 1973).

Olausson, Ulrika, 'Global warming — global responsibility? Media frames of collective action and scientific certainty', *Public Understanding of Science,* 18(4) (2009), 421–436.

Pietikäinen, Sari, 'Indigenous Identity in Print: Representations of the Sámi in News Discourse', *Discourse and Society,* 14(5) (2003), 581–609, http://dx.doi.org/10.1177/09579265030145003

—, 'Sámi in the Media: Questions of Language Vitality and Cultural Hybridization', *Journal of Multicultural Discourses,* 3(1) (2008), 22–35, http://dx.doi.org/10.2167/md088.0

Postman, Neil, *Amusing Ourselves to Death: Public Discourse in the Age of Show Business* (New York: Viking, 1985).

—, 'The Humanism of Media Ecology', *Proceedings of the Media Ecology Association,* 1(1) (2000), 10–16.

Roosvall, Anna, 'Media and Nationalism', in *The Wiley-Blackwell Encyclopaedia of Race, Ethnicity, and Nationalism,* ed. by John Stone, Rutledge M. Dennis, Polly R. Rizova, Anthony Smith and Xiaoshuo Hou (Oxford: John Wiley & Sons, 2016), pp. 1–4, http://dx.doi.org/10.1002/9781118663202.wberen274

—, and Tegelberg, Matthew, 'Media and the Geographies of Climate Justice: Indigenous Peoples, Nature and the Geopolitics of Climate Change', *Triple: Communication, Capitalism & Critique,* 13(1) (2015), 39–54.

—, and Tegelberg, Matthew, 'Framing Climate Change and Indigenous Peoples: Intermediaries of Urgency, Spirituality and De-Nationalization', *International Communication Gazette,* 75(1) (2013), 392–409, http://dx.doi.org/10.1177/1748048513482265

—, and Tegelberg, Matthew, 'Misframing the Messenger: Scales of Justice, Traditional Ecological Knowledge and Media Coverage of Indigenous Peoples and Climate Change', in *Media Meets Climate: The Global Challenge for Journalism,* ed. by Elisabeth Eide and Risto Kunelius (Gothenburg: Nordicom, 2012), pp. 297–312.

Rose, Gillian, *Visual Methodologies. An Introduction to Researching with Visual Materials* (London: Sage Publications, 2011).

Russell, Adrienne, 'Myth and the Zapatista Movement: Exploring a Network Identity', *New Media & Society,* 7(4) (2005), 559–577, http://dx.doi.org/10.1177/1461444805054119

Scolari, Carlos A., 'Media Evolution: Emergence, Dominance, Survival and Extinction in the Media Ecology', *International Journal of Communication,* 7(1) (2013), 1418–1441.

Suzuki, David, *The Sacred Balance: Rediscovering Our Place in Nature* (Toronto: Greystone Books, 1997).

Tauli-Corpuz, Victoria, 'Introduction', in *Guide on Climate Change and Indigenous Peoples*, ed. by Victoria, Tauli-Corpuz and de Chavez, Raymond (Baguio City: Tebtebba Foundation, 2009), pp. v-vii.

—, 'Adapting to Climate Change: Indigenous Peoples Show the Way', in *Guide on Climate Change and Indigenous Peoples*, ed. by Victoria Tauli-Corpuz and Raymond de Chavez (Baguio City: Tebtebba Foundation, 2009), pp. 35–42.

Tipa, Gail, 'Exploring Indigenous Understandings of River Dynamics and River Flows: A Case from New Zealand', *Environmental Communication: A Journal of Nature and Culture*, 3(1) (2009), 95–120, http://dx.doi.org/10.1080/17524030802707818

Tracy, Christine, 'A Quantum Exploration of the News Ecosystem', *Explorations in Media Ecology*, 9(3) (2010), 193–198.

—, 'Ecological Journalism and the Role of Perception', *Explorations in Media Ecology*, 11(2) (2012), 131–142, http://dx.doi.org/10.1386/eme.11.2.131_1

Urry, John, *Climate Change and Society* (Cambridge: Polity, 2011).

Van Dijk, Teun, 'New(s) Racism: A Discourse Analytical Approach', in *Ethnic Minorities and the Media*, ed. by Simon Cottle (Buckingham: Open University Press, 2000), pp. 33–49.

—, *News as Discourse* (New Jersey: Lawrence Erlbaum Associates, 1988).

Witschge, Tamara, and Nygren, Gunnar, 'Journalism: A Profession under Pressure?', *Journal of Media Business Studies*, 6(1) (2009), 37–59.

5. The Culture of Nature: The Environmental Communication of Gardening Bloggers

Heike Graf

This chapter examines 'ordinary' people's media communication about environmental issues. I have chosen the example of garden blogs. They fall under the category of topic-centred blogs; themes concerning gardens and gardening are expected and communicated through narratives, comments, and images. Based on approximately fifty Swedish and German blogs and a qualitative, difference-theoretical analysis, I want to examine how they communicate ecological concerns from the angle of gardeners' everyday 'banalities'. To this end, I examine the communicative patterns which increase the likelihood of interconnected communication within the blogosphere, patterns which, in turn, create virtual collectives, and can support ecological roles in the garden. Blog entries relate to the blog's own mode of operation and that of its network, meaning that the topics addressed are those that have the potential quality of 'embracing' all the people interested in the network. As a result, blog entries addressing ecological concerns focus on topics of *consumption* and *production* through the communication frames of pleasure, enthusiasm, and mutual agreement.

   http://dx.doi.org/10.11647/OBP.0096.05

Garden Blogs

Blogging has been described as a publishing revolution, and has become, as a result, a topic of interest within media research. The bulk of existing blog research focuses on issues such as the relationships between bloggers and the public sphere, or bloggers and journalism in order to understand the increasing influence of weblog authors on public opinion. Researchers have also addressed gender and identity issues, as well as media genre issues, educational purposes, and relationships within blog communities (e.g., Gurak et al. 2004; Lopez 2009; Lüders et al. 2010; Pole 2010; van Doorn et al. 2007; Schmidt 2007; Siles 2012).

Garden blogs, however, belong to the sphere of domestic blogs. Compared to other domestic blogs, such as craft, fashion, and interior décor blogs, the presence of garden blogs on the Internet is still relatively limited (Bosch Studie 2011). According to the commercial study *Global Garden Report 2010*, gardening blogging is popular in Scandinavia (as well as in the USA, UK, and China), but less popular in the German-speaking countries (the study mentions Austria and Switzerland, and presumably it also applies to Germany). Swedish gardening bloggers are largely women, as noted in the report. There are no statistics on German gardening bloggers, but here I would also assume that most of the bloggers are women.

The oldest garden blog, written in Swedish, originated in 2005, but most blogging activity has occurred since 2008, and most blogs are situated within a blog host, such as blogspot.com. Often in the form of a diary, one engages in the act of blogging when they add 'posts' to their weblog. They give insight to their thoughts and post pictures for others, allowing their audience to read these entries and provide feedback through enabled comment functions.

Approximately 50 more-or-less regularly updated garden blogs, 25 written in Swedish and 25 in German, comprised this study. In selecting the blogs, I used criteria, such as identifying hobby gardeners, that catch a certain variety of popular and somewhat popular blogs; gender is also a criterion, although most garden bloggers are female. Of the examined blogs, 50% were created by females, 30% by men, and 20% by couples. Finally, the examined garden bloggers are ordinary people who possess a small or large garden to cultivate vegetables, fruits, trees, and flowers. Since it is their hobby, they mostly garden for pleasure. In line with many other bloggers, they see blogging as an activity pursued for enjoyment (Lenhart 2006, 7).

The blogs selected for this study are a mixture of well-established and more recent blogs, with differing numbers of frequent readers (e.g., subscribers on blogspot.com). Some of these blogs attract from 50 to 400 followers, with others drawing more than 1,000 visitors per month. Depending on the type and intensity of the prevailing network, Jan Schmidt (2006) distinguishes between strong and weak ties. Strong ties are characterised by manifold relationships, for instance, knowing someone not only from virtual life but also from 'real' life, as a friend and/or relative. Looking at the comments on the entries, it is often obvious that relatives and/or close friends follow the entries. These ties make it easier to express solidarity and to give emotional support within virtual network communication. In contrast, weak ties mainly serve as information exchange, and in some ways establish mutual influence. According to Schmidt, those actors who are heavily involved in networks and their participants are also connected to each other, and have a 'bonding social capital' (Schmidt 2006, 52).

I do not want to examine what the blogs are about so much as how they address ecological issues (see also recent articles by Haider 2015, and Smith 2015), and how they are shaped in order to increase the likelihood of interconnected communication. Thus, and according to systems theory as described below, I examine the own mode of operation of the blogosphere in order to understand how ecological issues find resonance (see the foreword in this volume), or not, in the blogosphere.

To answer my research question, I first made a list of all the topics addressed in each blog. Second, I sorted out the topics that did not deal with ecological issues. And third, I took a closer look at the topics that remained to understand how they are *conditioned* (a term I explain below). At first glance, the use of images differs. Hence, I divide the blogs into two types: (1) images, especially photos used as illustrations of texts, which represents approximately two-thirds of the examined blogs; and (2) photos that constitute the main content of the blog, which is then called a photo blog.

I have remained outside of this blogosphere as a 'lurker', that is, as a passive audience member. However, I have had access to posted comments when they were openly published. The entries that I analyse were posted between 2007 and 2014.

Environmental Communication from a Systems-Theoretical Perspective

This chapter is based on the theoretical perspective of operational constructivism, which considers posted content as always the result of a selection process of possible entries and images made by an observer, not by the world itself. Here, the observer perspective becomes central. Observing is complex and related to the own mode of operation, that is, to oneself, the content of the perceived information or undertaken activity, and also to the perceived blogosphere as such. It is a construction of meaning made by an observer and, therefore, contingent. But it is not arbitrary, and it is influenced by expectations, preconditions, and finally by what one's own consciousness and perception provide for meaning production (Luhmann 1987, 217).

According to this approach, the non-human environment, i.e. nature, can only be a subject when it is communicated about in the manner described in the introduction to this volume. According to Niklas Luhmann, we take notice of nature when we are irritated or disturbed by it in some way. This communicative *reaction* is called *resonance*. By means of our own modes of operation, we try to react to those disturbances. For example, the garden blogger presents methods of getting rid of pests, as I will show below.

In different contexts or (in the terminology of systems theory) different systems, communication can only be addressed according to communicative patterns society, or the blogosphere, or the media have established. In the news media, for example, communication about ecology in general and sustainability in particular is mainly associated with problems and dangers (e.g., Foust et al. 2009).

Difference-Theoretical Approach

Systems theory begins with a difference and not with a 'unity, a cosmology, a concept of the world or of being' (Luhmann 2013, 44). Difference means that one indicates one thing rather than another. It derives from the observer's perspective, which builds on differences. Observing means to draw distinctions. Difference also applies to the definition of systems. We cannot speak of systems without recognising that they are separated from something, that is, from their environment. For example, it is not possible to speak of blogging if we cannot distinguish it from other forms of communication. On the basis of this separation, the system, and here the blogosphere, obtains its unity and therefore the possibility to operate on its own. As a result, systems are operationally closed, but must also be sensitive to the general environments in which they function. They cannot exist without an environment.

Systems theory avoids essentialism. It maintains that the world itself does not contain any information. For example, a blog entry about the benefits of wildflower-rich lawns says more about the blogger's sense-making than about the actual lawn. 'Information is information *for* an observer' (Fuchs 2001, 17). It is not information if the observer cannot *connect* to it. To connect to it, the observation must mean something to an observer (in my case to the blogger). This applies to both those who write blogs, and to those who read them.

If we apply a difference-theoretical approach to my field of study, we have to admit that we cannot say anything about what the blog-writing gardener really does in the garden — even if the blog is decorated with a lot of garden images and seems to display the garden's reality. However, we can say something about the relationship of the gardener-observer to that which he or she observes. As I have argued elsewhere (Graf 2012), it becomes obvious that the blog entries we examine are related to the blogger's preferences, to the blog as a genre and as a network, and to the various social systems to which the blog topics refer.

Differences can already be seen with the choice of blog name. One might call one's blog simply 'André's Blog', or, more programmatically, 'The Optimistic Gardener', or even 'Northern bliss'. Often, a blog will feature a motto that further articulates its specific identity, such as 'For an unhappy person, every flower is a weed, for a happy one, each weed is a flower' (Das wilde Gartenblog). They my also feature a brief description such as 'Thoughts and reflections about the gardens, the dirt under the fingernails, and a little chatter' (Fundera Grönt, see Figure 5.1).

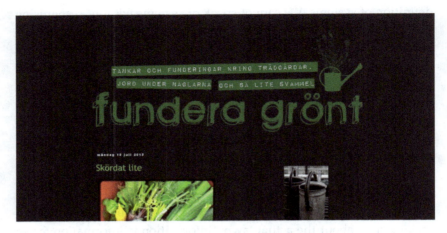

Fig. 5.1: The motto of this blog: 'Thoughts and reflections about the gardens, the dirt under the fingernails, and a little chatter' (http://funderagront.blogspot.se)

On the 'About Me' pages, one often finds self-descriptions and sometimes even a photo of the blogger. Some bloggers divulge their own or their garden's address in order to give information about specific gardening conditions, while others, more reticent, only mention their gender and the region where they live or where the garden is situated (see Graf 2012).

Blogging is intentional; the entries must possess 'connectivity', if communication is to occur. According to Luhmann (1987), communication is not the transmission of information, but the union of three components: the selection of information (what is selected to be communicated or what the message is about), the selection of utterance (of a form of communication: how the information is to be communicated), and the selection of understanding (about the meaning that is generated: is a meaning selected, and if so which one?). Connectivity is determined by the contact or relationship with something, in our case the blogosphere, that *condition* communication in terms of what is possible in concrete communication practices. Without these conditions, meaningful blog communication would not be possible.

The blog entries create a chain of operations, and this happens selectively. The chain already begins with the information. Information is — in line with its standard definition (cf. Shannon and Weaver

1949) — a selection from a repertoire of possibilities. In other words, it is a selection made to communicate this and not other information. For example, on the right side column of the website we can find a list of self-determined blog categories such as 'Weeds', 'Friday', 'Watery', etc. We can also find automatically generated links to older entries, and links to other blogs and an archive of older posts. Furthermore, Luhmann's communication hypothesis includes the issue of *how* to communicate this selected information. There is a clear difference between information and utterance. One can decorate the blog's posted information with images; one can express the information in different rhetorical styles, in different languages, etc. What is more, information plus utterance may not get anyone's attention (in which case the communication does not take place). Conversely, information plus utterance can be understood (in which case communication does take place). Here, understanding is not a psychological concept. We are not concerned with what a message or the author behind the message really mean. However, communication within the blogosphere, for instance, occurs when a reaction takes place, that is, when blog entries or comments 'relate' to each other (Taekke 2005, 14). For example, some kind of understanding is indicated by the statistics appearing on the right-hand column of the blog: a list of subscribers, the numbers of visitors per day, including the countries from which the visitors come, and a list of links to other blogs and websites. However, it is in the connecting communication (that is, comments, entries referring to other entries, etc.) that understanding first takes place — a clear differentiation between information and utterance is made.

The central problem of being able to understand information and utterance — that is, being *connectible* in the communication process — is that communication is only understandable in context. In this respect, communication processes are always formed by the observer's expectations and his or her commonly shared knowledge. Because of the dependence on contexts, communication is bound to concrete environments, to places and times. Every communicative contribution within a discourse is verified whether or not it is relevant or expected. One can use one's own experience to set up communication in such a way that one may expect to be understood (Luhmann 1987, 140).

The act of indicating something tells us where we are and where we might continue (Luhmann 2013, 54). In indicating, for example, that organic food is more desirable than conventional food, a blogger reveals how *irritations* from the non-human environment as well as the social environment (e.g., politics, media, economy, family) are processed within the genre of blogging. Applying systems theory demands thinking in relationships; meaning that the treatment of a topic about food is not arbitrary, but limited in different ways. All communication has its own mode and its own common sense. Commonality is limited by garden bloggers' modes and *hows*, and not by contents and *whats*, as I will show in the following sections.

The Role of Topics

Generally, communication occurs with the help of topics. In other words, topics are the essential precondition for communication, and represent what can be of interest to others according to one's own mode of communication. Topics combine different utterances and thereby structurally link the blogosphere. In addition, they organise the memory of communication (Luhmann 1996, 28). Without posting topics there can be no network of bloggers.

As mentioned above, blog postings on ecology can be generally understood as *resonance* (Luhmann 2008), that is, bloggers resonate in reaction to *irritations* caused by the natural environment or by the way in which the social environment deals with ecological dangers. The success of a blogosphere depends on the acceptance of the bloggers' topics. Bloggers thus depend on people giving them attention by reacting to them with communication of their own.

Not all topics are successful: some are ignored. Some topics, however, provoke new contributions or entries in the blogosphere over and over again. Schmidt (2006) differentiates between topics that are 'spikes', 'spiky chatters', and 'mostly chatters'. The first are topics which attract only limited attention from observers; the second are wave-like, as they are discussed over a longer period; and the third set of topics are discussed at a low but stable level (Schmidt 2006, 58).

Topics have a concrete or factual aspect on the one hand, and a temporal one on the other. Here, according to Luhmann, we can distinguish between topics and contributions (Luhmann 1996, 28f). In the blogosphere, contributions are called posts or entries. These entries refer to topics and can take the form of images or textual messages. Topics live longer than the individual posts do, and combine the different posts into a long-term or short-term nexus of meaning. Some posts provoke new contributions or at least comments. However, other topics are exhausted quickly.

The observer (and in this case the blogger) can distinguish between topics and functions of communication. For example, he or she can say to him or herself and to others: if I do not explain this or that in a special way, I will end up losing my followers. This reasoning has to do with the underlying mode of communication which is both connected to social values (e.g., environmental behaviour) and to the rules of the blogosphere (see Graf 2012). I will explain this further when dealing with the various topics.

According to news value research, and in a similar way to mass media, the blog entries follow certain selection criteria with regard to information and utterance. These criteria also influence how the information is posted. As I have written elsewhere, selection criteria such as novelty, values, identification, conflicts, and visuality guide garden bloggers' communication (Graf 2012). For example, an entry has to tell us something new. The simple repetition of a previous entry is not expected. The issue of ecology is associated with known values such as sustainability or biodiversity, and referring to them can presuppose common acceptance and facilitate understanding. In addition, blogging about a hobby such as gardening involves feelings and emotions which facilitate the identification with an entry and therefore connective communication.

Ecology and Gardening in the Mainstream Media

Blogging about the garden does not occur in a vacuum. It is influenced to a great extent by the mass media's coverage of ecology, that is, of the human relations with the non-human environment. With the help of anxiety rhetoric, the news media´s coverage revolves around problems and dangers. Over time, it has become common sense to communicate in favour of doing something to combat global warming, pollution, ozone depletion, deforestation, etc.

In contrast to news journalism, anxiety rhetoric plays a subordinated role in TV programs, and magazines covering lifestyle and hobby issues such as gardening. Gardens as 'artificial creations within Nature' (Verdi 2004, 361) have always been of human interest and, hence, a topic for literature, fine and applied arts, science, TV programs, etc. Communicating about gardens and gardening is rich in symbols as well as feelings: gardening offers both a spiritual and a physical dimension, and can be interpreted in practical and also decorative ways. It can also be communicated as a place of politics (McKay 2011; Graf 2014). The aim of the gardener often relates to the Garden of Eden trope: all modern gardeners are 'engaged in recapturing Eden, if only in a limited way, and some more explicitly than others' (Nadel-Klein 2010, 167).

Content about garden and gardening has enjoyed high popularity in the last twenty years. In line with lifestyle media (Christensen 2008), the media presentation of gardening deals with people's spare time, where the demands of the working life are absent. It focuses on dreams of greater well-being, and shows how these dreams can bee realised. Readers and viewers are told what to do in their gardens in order to improve their quality of life. TV programs and garden magazines focus on consumers' desire for the new and try to feed it; one learns how to renew the garden in order to make it more tasteful. Readers and viewers are informed about the latest goods to purchase in order to be 'attuned to the culturally befitting ways of how they should be consumed' (Taylor 2005, 123). The garden is seen as a paradise won in 'the struggle against the overpower of Nature', and as 'Nature tamed and made elegant, a far cry from dark and dangerous thorny forests or deserts' (Verdi 2004, 361, 363).

Gardens have become a place where issues of identity can be expressed. To renew one's garden has to do with positioning oneself in regard to symbolic values. These lifestyle media insist that the 'aestheticisation of components of everyday life — such as the garden — will lead to a more gratifying lifestyle' (Taylor 2005, 123). In these makeover programs and magazines, a rapid lifestyle benefit is simulated, while principles of what is considered to be good taste and style are simultaneously disseminated. Thus, gardening is seen from the angle of pure appearance and exhibited 'as a desirable end in itself' (Taylor 2005, 119). Images of the perfect garden adorn the pages of glossy magazines, which Taylor describes as promoting an 'almost clinic obsession with maintaining a coherent design' (Taylor 2005, 119), often without consideration of climate and location.

This trend of expanding aesthetics to the non-social environment has gained momentum in the last past ten years. It is also connected to a kind of 'ecological turn', as Lyn Thomas (2008, 177) has observed of British lifestyle television, where *irritations* deriving both from the non-human and social environment are addressed. It is not only about the pure beauty of village and garden life, but also about destructive habits of consumption that must be changed. The 'ecoreality' of British lifestyle programs defines a new morality aimed at changing our way of living. It emphasises individual solutions, such as a sustainable way of life, rather than mere style and appearance (Thomas 2008). Television gardening supports the dissemination of ethical information by providing advice on how to garden in an ecological manner (Bonner 2008, 31). Thus, design and sustainability need not be contradictions. Business has jumped on the bandwagon and begun to mark their products as environmentally friendly. Purchasing organic or locally produced food has become part of the green zeitgeist. Growing one's own carrots and cabbages nicely planted together with edible flowers might also involve pleasure and the projection of a pleasing appearance. Reducing one's lawn with insect-friendly flowers in order to halt the decline in honey bees and insect pollinators can also improve the fashionableness of the garden; such horticultural knowledge and good taste can impress one's friends and visitors. Here, tasteful design does not come above all else, but it is supported by the moral values of environmentally friendly practice in the garden. This can go even further in other (e.g., Australian) gardening shows, where water-wise gardening is central to dealing with permanent water scarcity. Therefore, aesthetics is no longer of major consideration, as Frances Bonner suggests: 'Regardless of pleasing appearance, good gardening here produces fruits and vegetables, especially tomatoes' (Bonner 2008, 32). Going green is fashionable, and marks a certain modern lifestyle.

To summarise, the content of media programs and magazines about gardens and gardening may vary, and offer something for everyone. One can enjoy a total makeover show and feel the desire to do the same or at least purchase new goods for one's immediate pleasure; or one can observe garden design informed by ecological implications and at least consider rejecting thoughts on fashionableness.

The Topics of Gardening Blogs

With the rise of the Internet, gardening issues are no longer reserved for the mass media but can also be addressed by individual people to a large public. Similar to the treatment of the above mentioned topics in the media, the communicative reactions of the garden bloggers to ecological concerns cohere around two ideas: domination over or partnership with nature. As such, the entries generally concentrate on two main topics: topics of *consumption* in terms of goods, and topics of *production* in terms of gardening.

The discussion of these topics is stable and sometimes even wave-like. These are topics with a high potential of connectivity: most of the bloggers can and do refer to them frequently, and thus reveal what they think of the non-human environment. This means that if one wants to trigger further communication, ecological concerns, such as global warming, are not addressed in isolation but are folded into gardening issues (see Graf 2011, 276).

How the bloggers put themselves in a position to recognise ecological concerns in terms of these issues is a question that relates not only to the non-human and social environment but also to the blog as such, especially the role that photos play in the blog. If photos dominate the blog, garden life is mostly seen through the lens of a camera (Graf 2012). As a result, garden design and aesthetics are in focus, and ecological concerns may not interfere with pleasing appearances.

When addressing *consumption* issues, I will stress the fundamental distinction between controlled consumption and the unfettered purchasing typical of the market economy. I will not focus on consumption in terms of consuming the beauty of nature, as photo blogs mainly do, but consumption defined as consuming goods offered on the market. Hence, my examples stem from text-based blogs which include, e.g., advice to buy special garden products and not others. These types of reactions to *irritations* are mainly directed at the social environment, whereas topics about *production* are directed both at the social and non-social environment. The latter kind are generally about sustainable methods: green gardening that involves planting, improving, and preparing the soil, as well as garden aesthetics. Topics can deal with hands-on advice about ecological soil improvement and plant protection, and can also relate to reflections about appearance and biological diversity. Green gardening, especially pest control and biodiversity, is often addressed in relation to attitudes of respect (partnership) and disrespect (domination) towards nature.

Both topics have likely to arouse the expression of emotions and values, which function as identity markers in the blogosphere. This mixture of emotions and beliefs create a personal arena of expression in order to show what the garden means for the blogger, and a need to manage one's relations in the blogosphere.

In the following, I want to illustrate in detail how bloggers communicate ecological awareness (or the lack of it) according to the main topics of consumption and production. I will then draw conclusions about the mode of communication used in the blogosphere of garden bloggers.

Consumption: Developing/Refusing a 'Buyosphere'

Julia Corbett (2006) claims that the environmental lifestyle communicated by the marketplace is 'hedonistic and narcissistic — it's all about your enjoyment, your pleasure and comfort, about your looking good and having the latest toys' (2006, 93). Some of my examined bloggers adapt the semantics of hedonism and encourage consumption. They inform each other about the latest products and where to buy the cheapest plants. Hence, they create a 'buyosphere' (Corbett 2006, 93ff) in which bloggers use expressions like 'I want that' and 'It was a real steal', showing their gratitude for being inspired to purchase new products. This topic also contains complaints about insufficient space, from gardeners who cannot find room for the new plants they want to purchase.

Some personal bloggers also use targeted advertisements, have commercial sponsors, and aspire to commercialising their blogging activities. As a result, they promote their own and others' products and services, from food to design: many gardening bloggers advertise and sell their handicrafts. Besides showing commercial instincts, they all, to some degree, seem to be inspired by other posts presenting new products, plants, or garden tools. New purchases are sometimes ecologically motivated (in order to increase insect life in the garden, for example), and sometimes motivated entirely by a desire to consume.

This latter motivation is expressed the following example, in which a female blogger tells a success story about purchasing a coveted plant at a reduced price:

> This week I got a very good bargain. Was eating breakfast when I saw that they sold olive trees at City Gross. My dear colleague E was also excited so we set off with my van. We thought that they would already be sold since the ad had warned that they had only a very limited number of trees. (Landet krokus, 5 May 2011)

The blog is relatively popular, with 274 readers (May 2015), and can be credited with a certain bonding capital. In response to this post, the author received eleven comments which shared her excitement. The post (and the blog as a whole) emphasises garden style issues, with little consideration for location or climate. Possessing an olive tree, which seldom or never bears fruit in the Scandinavian climate, has a symbolic power of trendiness in the consumer society. Olive trees are associated with the Mediterranean — that is, with leisure time, relaxation and a feel-good atmosphere. The identity-value of the tree overshadows its use-value. In addition to a plant, the blogger has also bought style and an appearance of trendiness, which can be displayed to the blogosphere.

However, the purchase of an olive tree does not mean the same thing to all gardeners, as revealed in a comment from another female blogger, rated lower with respect to followers, at 74 (May 2015):

> Mediterranean flair is this year's catchphrase in the garden world [...] and the shops follow suit. 129kr for a 1.5m-tall olive tree at a discount store. Have not fallen for it yet. Olive trees will soon be in the home of every Svensson, worth her name, I guess. Like the new harangue: house, dog, and an olive tree. (Trädgårdstankar, 12 May 2011)

In adopting trends, this blogger makes a distinction: once the olive tree becomes part of mass-lifestyle culture, the blogger loses interest, since it can no longer be the vehicle of an individualised vision of herself. Bargains help to spread a sort of mass-culture of gardening, which this blogger rejects. There is only one comment on this post saying,

> Olive tree [...] yes I have two and I'm getting sick of them, do not really believe it's my thing. They do not look so nice if I may say so. (Trädgårdstankar comment, 17 May 2011)

To follow garden trends is to find intense, short-lived pleasure in novelties. The implication is that one changes plants each season. This kind of interest in plants produces a consumer attitude which entails constant renewal. Another blogger criticises this attitude:

> Not enough that the fashion industry forces us to critically see over our closet year after year, now even the flower industry can give us a bad conscience. The potted plants trend is away from small-scale flowers, bustling flower windows, to huge soloists, the bigger the better […] I have better things to do than following every trend according to potted plants. (Günstig gärtnern, 28 Jan 2011)

This female blogger refuses to apply an ideology of trendiness to houseplants, and thus to adopt a lifestyle culture which demands a 'rapid turnover of identity indicators' (Bonner 2008, 34). The fifteen responses to her post all agree with this sentiment, tell different stories on the same theme, and stress the incompatibility of sustainability and fashionable gardening trends. These trends lead to throw-away thinking, which in turn exhausts natural resources and causes ecological damage. Most of the responses stress the importance of establishing a relationship to one's own plants, a view that is incompatible with ephemeral fashion. Close relationships with plants, and with nature, is a recurring theme in blogs that favour sustainable gardening over trend-following and constant renewal (Graf 2011). These entries show, in line with nature identification research (e.g., Milstein 2011), that nature identification practices can shape ecological roles and, more concretely, lead to the rejection of unfettered consumption.

A more ecocentric perspective is taken, for example, in complaints about 'careless container planting'. The containers hold plants with differing light and water requirements; these plants are selected exclusively for the sake of their decorative foliage and flowers. Here, appearance takes precedence over good growing conditions. These containers are made for a quick sale, and have short life-spans, which in turn causes people purchase more of them. This throw-away culture, which has spread to garden products, gives a wider perspective on the society we live in, as this blogger relates:

> For me, it is simply an emerging disregard towards nature. I go so far as to say that these little things contribute to the growing disrespect shown

to people in many ways [...] For negative things always begin creeping, in small format. (Wurzels Garten, 19 Aug 2007)

This entry received nine responses, all of which expressed approval, e.g., 'it's nice to know that there are like-minded people' (Wurzels Garten, 19 August 2007). Commentators recount similar observations, and at the same time they ask self-critically if the gardening blogosphere is free from 'sins against nature' such as 'thoughtlessly consuming' the garden products on offer. This comment, emphasising individual behaviour, demands that bloggers take a critical look at their own consumer behaviour.

Another object of criticism is the economy of abundance, with displays of a growing number of gardening products and accessories. According to this next female blogger, who has 113 followers (June 2013), such displays are unnecessary:

> Currently, DIY stores, garden centres, supermarkets, and even drugstores accumulate garden accessories. The seed trays, pots, seedling transplant tools, peat pots. There are heated green houses and 'root trainer' for vegetables, tomato supports of all kind of materials, and for each seedling you can find the respective pot and fluid. In addition there are kneepads, huge collections of gardeners clothing from shoes to hats, gloves and garden jackets; vegetable and seed labels from wood, metal or plastic for hanging, plugging and clamping. This is really astonishing because nobody really needs those things [...]. (Mauerblumen, 30 March 2011)

As an alternative to buying new products, the blogger shows her readers how to reuse old tin cans or even baking pans for planting seeds, how to build one's own mini-greenhouse with plastic bottles which have been cut, and how to use plastic wraps to keep the soil moist in indoor seed beds. Finally, she admonishes her followers and readers not to buy 'all this stupid stuff!' This is different from the previous blogger's discussion of the olive tree. Industry's attempt to infuse these products with meaning and link them to lifestyle has not succeeded here. Rather, the attempt provoked a blog entry that argues for critical consumption and against purchasing unnecessary goods. The blogger received nine comments describing similar experiences of unnecessary purchasing and contributing further advice about how to reuse materials. All the commentators argue, in effect, that one must take use-value into account when purchasing something.

This topic of abstinence from consumption includes contributions about various liquid solutions for creating the 'perfect garden', such as 'lawn without moss' and 'flower beds without weeds'. As one entry argues:

> When you are in the store you will be easily convinced that there are the herbicides you just need. What you cannot read on the leaflet is that this disrupts the micro life of the soil and may even damage the plants you want to protect. (Lindas Trädgårdsblogg, 11 April 2011)

This blogger, who has 137 followers (May 2015), warns against buying chemical fertilisers and moss killing products. All eight responses express approval. The writers thank her for a wise blog entry and highlight critical consumer behaviour by telling similar stories.

The range of garden products is also critiqued from the perspective of 'respect' for nature. Such respect is indicative of the favoured relationship between humans and nature, one which Merchant describes 'as a partnership rather than domination' (Merchant 2003, 206). For example, one blogger, with 105 followers (December 2013), gives information about the conditions in which the poinsettia, which is very popular at Christmas time, is produced. The writer quotes from the Swedish Nature Conservation Society, enlightening the reader with information about the large amount of pesticides used in poinsettia production. These pesticides are harmful to people, especially to those who grow them, and to the environment. This observation leads to a clear statement:

> If the merchant cannot guarantee toxic-free poinsettias, there will be a Christmas without them. (Njut i Din Trädgård, 14 December 2010)

All six responders agree and demand more information about the conditions under which popular house-plants are grown. The idea is to make the consumer more informed and critical.

These entries, in turn, inspire a whole range of entries about what to buy and what not to buy in order to undertake ecological gardening. This work should begin with the selection of the right seeds, as an entry makes clear:

> It feels really good to buy organic seeds when I want to grow organically. My little garden is microscopic compared to the area that is used to

produce the seeds! If I then choose to buy organic seeds, it should make a little difference? (Lindas Trädgårdsblogg, 22 March 2012)

The process may continue with, for instance, the resolution to buy heirloom seeds and plants instead of hybrids in order to preserve biodiversity. The reader learns that heirloom seeds are, in contrast to the hybrids, open-pollinated.

A great many entries are about purchasing the right food, meaning food that is ecological and locally grown. The following blogger, who has 465 subscribed readers (May 2015) and thus a certain amount of bonding social capital in the Swedish blogosphere, challenges his blog audience to cook with organic food. His ambition is to involve and engage the whole network, making them think and act ecologically:

> By the way, today, it will be 100% organic. It feels a little better each time I do this. I'm still not 100% organic in my life, but on the way […] If you think this is a hard task, it is because I am just a thorn in your side and you wish that you could make this decision, too. Yep it is so! (Hannu På Kinnekulle, 10 May 2011)

This blogger also thinks it necessary to change consumer behaviour. Judging from the comments, he meets with approval: some readers want to do better, some tell him they already eat organic food, and so on. A few weeks later, he returns to the subject, telling his audience that he feels good when buying locally produced organic food. He documents the claim with a photo of his freshly purchased goods (19 September 2011). He also relates how he declines to buy certain products, such as his favourite salami sausage, because the store cannot offer organic alternatives:

> […] something strange happened then, I said no thanks and left without buying my favourites, hm. I've never done it before. But I'm in an organic mood that I hope lasts for a long time; a vegetarian doesn't munch a grilled beef tenderloin just because there's no salad! (Hannu På Kinnekulle, 10 April 2010)

Other bloggers argue in favour of ecological meat. However, not all locally produced meat is ecological, which one blogger finds regrettable:

> Unfortunately, not everything they sell is KRAV labelled (organic production), but most of it is locally produced. We are trying to cut down on our consumption of meat (especially beef), but it feels good to

buy from local farms where the cattle have grazed in the neighbourhood. Then it also feels good to be able to show the kids where the food we eat comes from. (Lindas Trädgårdsblogg, 8 March 2012)

As these examples illustrate, ecological issues, understood as reactions to *irritations* caused by the market economy, are, under the topic of consumption, addressed from a great variety of perspectives. One can argue for both more or less consumption, and even for boycotting consumption. One can introduce values to the conversation and argue for the right or wrong way of consuming. Thus good roles, that is to say critical consumer attitudes, are mostly articulated from the point of view of one's own behaviour (Graf 2012), and bad roles are mostly ascribed to the market economy with its drive for profit and destructive influence on the non-human environment. One can further introduce emotions in order to strengthen one's own argument. By attributing values and norms to consumer behaviour, a social dimension of communication is actualised. It can, for example, be expressed as 'green' behaviour and related to the *zeitgeist*; to a greater or lesser degree, this is what creates bonds between bloggers in the network.

Why do bloggers so often describe objects of consumption either as something that they 'must have' or something that should be boycotted? It is common knowledge that consumption issues dominate our lives. Many scholars describe modern society as a consumption society, in which to live means first and foremost to consume (e.g., Bauman 2007, Hellmann 2011). Nevertheless, not all acts of consumption are subjects of communication. Why do gardening bloggers busy themselves in addressing these issues?

Consumption studies have shown that individual choice has increased to such an extent that every form of consumption is contingent and therefore based on a decision about what to select (Hellmann 2011, 220). The decision-making process increases the possibility of communicating about consumption. What function does the topic of consumption have within the blogosphere? Again, it is about managing relations: how do bloggers wish to be regarded by others? They express identity, and therefore preferences, in accordance with the roles they assume in the blogosphere. Some bloggers prefer to blog about recycling possibilities and to show their creativity in finding new solutions. Some prefer to blog about the latest fashionable plant they purchased, in order to mark their affiliation to a certain group of 'modern', trendy people. Others prefer to do both.

The consumption issue involves feelings and fantasies and offers a wide spectrum of topics to communicate about. Goods can be ascribed symbolic meanings and ranked according to aesthetic criteria. The view of an olive tree in the garden can start someone daydreaming, which can then lead to a blog entry about the great feeling of having got a good deal in purchasing the plant. Communication about consumption issues ensures that all readers are more or less involved and hence interested — that is, it is a topic that 'embraces everyone' (Slater cit. in Hellmann 2011, 242) and so increases the possibility of connective communication.

Production: Developing Green Gardening

Gardeners' blogs about improving the soil by growing organically, being sparing with natural resources such as water, and avoiding the use of pesticides for pest control are embedded in an array of ecological concerns. I have not read a single post advocating the use of pesticides or chemical fertilisers in order to get a bigger harvest. My educated guess is that if some bloggers were using pesticides, they would not write about it. One male blogger did a poll among his followers, asking how many used synthetic fertilisers and pesticides: 39 bloggers answered, of whom 64% never used these products, while 36% did (Wir Sind im Garten, 31 January 2010). However, it seems an unwritten rule that the network communication of gardening bloggers mainly revolves around some form of green gardening. Posting a statement in favour of pesticides would cause the blogger to lose followers. Accordingly, there is a recurring pattern among gardening bloggers of making clear statements like the following:

> For me, it is obvious not to use toxins or chemical fertilisers. I want the garden to grow from a land where worms and microorganisms feel comfortable. I like the idea of having a cycle in the garden where I use plant remains and grass clippings that become soil, which I can then grow in. To disrupt the soil ecosystem with environmental toxics does not feel good. (Lindas Trädgårdsblogg, 14 April 2011)

She received eight responses, all of which were positive; some thanked her for making the statement, and wanted to follow her example.

Nevertheless, gardening is not without disturbances. A great number of entries are about pest control; for example, what should one do when the Spanish slug invades the garden? Here again, entries suggesting non-toxic methods are at the forefront. Much advice is given: different sorts of traps are shown and their function explained — beer traps, overturned flowerpots, grapefruit halves left overnight, or coffee grounds placed on the top of the soil to protect plants against attacks. Where this invasive slug is concerned, entries often express negative emotions and describe vivid behaviour, as the following female blogger shows:

> Jahapp, so, it is time again. May I present: The first Spanish slug! This brazen creature has dared to show up on my terrace [...] Immediately, I went back into the house and took a pair of pincers and a small plastic bag. Went for a walk in the garden and got together a small bag of 'good & mixed' that I put in the freezer. I think, it is the easiest and least messy way to get rid of slugs. Obviously, it should be the least painful, too. After few days in the freezer they have fallen asleep forever and you can throw the bag in the trash. (Trädgårdstoken, 11 June 2010, see Figure 5.2)

Fig. 5.2 The first Spanish slug in the garden (Trädgårdstoken, http://www. tradgardstoken.se/2010/06/sniglar.html)

To most of the bloggers, discovering the first slug is an inducement to write about different ways of killing them. This meets with approval. It is considered fair to kill slugs, if the deed is performed in a manner that causes a minimum of suffering. One male blogger compares his slug killing with the 'massacre' at Wounded Knee and accompanies it with a photo of a pair of scissors next to bisected slugs (Nervenruh, 21 July 2011). Slugs, and especially Spanish slugs, give rise to loaded language and emotive arguments, which provoke further communication. Since these arguments mostly connect to shared, negative connotations, the expression of negative feelings is likely to meet with sympathy and further communication from the blog community. The topic of slugs has the potential function of allowing, and perhaps also directing, strong negative emotions in communication. Here, the line between respect and disrespect towards nature is drawn: in plain English, slugs do not deserve respect.

However, this sentiment does not apply to all bloggers. Under the heading 'One always does things differently', a female blogger, whose entries often show a clear identification with nature and an ecocentric point of view, describes her different way of dealing with pests:

> [...] I wish the slugs in my vegetable garden 'bon appétit!' instead of killing them, and I'm delighted to see all the happy weeds in the patio slab gaps. (Mauerblumen, 27 May 2011)

This blogger, who has 113 followers (June 2013), received six comments. None of them explicitly discuss her unconventional attitude towards slugs, but in a general manner they praise her 'individualism' and 'humorous writing style', accompanied by 'wonderful photos' of columbine flowers. However, the comments do not address the topic of slug control; on this subject there is no further communication. The garden blog community seems to agree: when it comes to pest control, there are limits to one's respect for nature.

When bloggers write about identification with, and respect for, nature, biodiversity is a recurring theme, especially where green gardening is concerned. This tendency can conflict with the recommended gardening methods. Two bloggers (a couple) prefer to leave dead trees standing in order to support a rich insect life.

We don't like to cut dead trees, if we can think of another use. Dead wood is good for small animals and can be an element to create structure in the garden. (Das wilde Gartenblog, 9 August 2010, see Figure 5.3)

Baumskelett als Rosenständer

9. August 2010 von ClaudiaBerlin

Das hier ist das Skelett eines Pfirsichbaums, der nach dem letzten Winter kein Lebenszeichen mehr von sich gegeben hatte. Schon zuvor trug er nur noch auf einigen wenigen Ästen Blätter und Früchte.

Fig. 5.3 A tree skeleton as trellis (das wilde Gartenblog, http://www.das-wilde-gartenblog.de/2010/08/09/baumskelett-als-rosenstaender)

This method is illustrated by the picture above, which shows the tree skeleton being used as a trellis. All four responses praise this 'great idea'. By explaining the importance of insect diversity, the bloggers defend this exceptional trellis against possible critique as an 'ugly' garden design. Here, forms of sustainable gardening function as a means for getting likes. Had the bloggers not explained the reasoning behind this trellis, they would probably not have provoked comments or further communication, since positive feedback is the norm in the gardening blogosphere (Graf 2012).

Another issue which leads to a discussion of style versus sustainability is the lawn issue, meaning the obsession with cultivating the perfect lawn. A female blogger asks provocatively:

What to do against the English lawn? No matter, what gardening magazine I open at this time — the very big topic is currently not only about spring flowers but also about the so-called 'English lawn': a dark green, dense turf, free from intruding plants such as flowers, herbs and different types of grass. There seems to be gardeners, who actually want to have a lawn in the garden that looks like artificial grass, is ecologically useless, and needs a lot of care and chemicals. (Mauerblumen, 3 April 2011)

This female blogger, who attracts attention by contradicting conventional views and styles of gardening (e.g., the usual method of dealing with slugs), gives advice about how to increase the biodiversity of a mono-cultural lawn. Of 13 comments, all but one agree with her, saying for instance that 'This is also an anathema to me!' They stress the beauty of flowering lawns and tell more stories about improving biodiversity.

Soil improvement is another topic that, because it raises controversy, gives rise to many entries. Pros and cons of different soil improvement measures are discussed, and each blogger can make claims regarding her/his successful method without losing face. When the subject of sustainability is discussed, relatively new soil improvement methods can be introduced, as in the following entry:

Constant watering is not our goal, neither to acquire tons of fertile soil from elsewhere. Both alternatives make little sense, ecologically. It costs money, and energy, and does not change the underlying problem. We rather continuously work to improve the soil in order to increase the humus component that better keep nutrients and moisture. (Das wilde Gartenblog, 2 June 2011)

These bloggers[1] (another couple), whose blog explicitly specialises in sustainable gardening, introduce a new form of soil improvement by using terra preta, that is, a mixture of charcoal, pottery shards, and organic material. The couple shows how to make terra preta and how to create a flower-bed using it. Their first results are displayed: vegetables that grow better than in ordinary beds.

All of the fifteen comments are positive, expressing gratitude for news of this innovative method of soil improvement and adding more information about it. The blog entry has something distinctive to tell that gets attention and evokes further communication.

---

1   There is no data on the number of people who follow this blog.

The preparation of garden beds is a topic that leads to discussions about whether the soil should be turned or not. There are two categories of entries, divided by their recommendations for preparing the soil. One group of entries claims that turning the soil is essential. Another group, which highlights sustainable gardening, holds the opposite position. The following entry belongs to this latter category:

> Good soil is ACTIVE (Living) — that is one that can develop a happy 'soil life' among microorganism, earth and plant roots. This would naturally be disturbed when one comes with a spade and turns it. (Das wilde Gartenblog, 10 November 2010)

This blog recommends mulching, in order to conserve moisture and improve the fertility of the soil. The entry provoked 16 comments, mostly expressing agreement. Only a few bloggers took into consideration the soil texture, and recommended digging in some cases, mainly when clay soil was in question. However, most of the commentators gave further reasons for mulching rather than digging, and added that this method saves energy and time for the gardener; they concluded that mulching is the best way to develop a healthy garden. In this blog, no divergent and competing opinions were expressed, even though there are possible alternative ways of improving the soil. By investing one's own descriptions of digging with values — in this case, that good soil means special digging practices — the blogger is attempting to direct the reader's understanding and invite his or her acceptance. Generally, values function on a basis of mutual agreement, that is, as long as they are not challenged. The comments that follow seem to indicate that this move has been successful: the entry is not challenged. But values can also be controversial, and the result can be a loss of readers and followers. Therefore, the addition of values to self-description is meant to direct communication, that is, manage it so that the blogosphere produces the desired relations, on the grounds of specific normative preferences. However, values have a limited range of application; they do not, for instance, give concrete instructions on how to deal with soil improvement under different conditions.

But not all bloggers communicate environmentally conscious gardening behaviour. As mentioned above, blogs dominated by photographic illustrations do not address environmental issues nearly as often, and if they do, environmental concerns are complemented by aesthetic considerations. In many cases, it matters little whether someone wants to cultivate a Mediterranean plant in a northern climate, or create a jungle atmosphere in a dry area by extensive watering. If one can present wonderful images from one's garden, one will gain respect and admiration in return.

The focal points of ecological concerns are primarily soil improvement, biodiversity, and pest control. In line with systems theory, the expression of green gardening behaviour can be understood as highly selective *resonance*, that is, as a reaction to bloggers' own ideas of what can be done in reaction to ecological danger. It conforms to the norms of the blogosphere with respect to subject matter and the manner of communication.

Conclusions

Blog entries are the outcome of a network of connected and related observations. They cannot be understood merely as *re*presentations of what is going on in the garden. There is a lot more to an entry. As a social means, entries must possess connectivity if communication is to occur. Hence, blogging has the function of managing relationships in the blogosphere, meaning that in the context of the blog community, communication is framed in such a way that entries are constantly coordinated with each other. By expressing preferences, a writer establishes a blog identity. The success of a blog depends on the acceptance of these uttered and visualised preferences. It means, that someone pays attention by reacting to the entries with further communication.

Topics belong to the precondition of communication. With respect to the examined garden bloggers, the most successful topics are those that have the quality of 'embracing' everyone interested in gardening and addressing ecology in some way, including issues of *consumption* and *production*. Addressed from the angle of gardening 'banalities', such blogs have the potential to enhance connecting communication. The content of the topics shows the *resonance*, that is, how the bloggers react to *irritations* of both the non-human and the social environment.

The topic of consumption can be addressed from several different perspectives; it is possible to argue for more or even less consumption without being aware of ecological consequences. However, topics concerned with production in home gardens are generally dominated by arguments for sustainable gardening, at least in text-based blogs.

How these topics find *resonance* in the blog entries relates — according to Luhmann — to the mode of operation that is particular to the blogosphere. In other words, references to ecological consequences such as climate change are seen from the point of view of the garden blogger, who is influenced by various preconditions, including his/her own consciousness, perception, and expectations of blog communication. To put this in concrete terms, *resonance* in the form of topics relates to the following communicative conditions understood as modes of operation:

The form of the blog: This is mainly determined by the use of images in the blogs. Photo blogs show gardening from an aesthetic, through-the-lens point of view. This produces a preference for constant renewal. Text-based blogs allow for more differentiation and, therefore, are more likely to display expressions of ecological awareness.

The blog identity: This defines the establishment of relationships. Blog relationships will be jeopardised if a blogger, in contrast to developed expectations of the blogger's views on consumption, biodiversity, ecological pest control, etc., transforms the blog into an environmentally unfriendly one, e.g., by arguing for the use of chemical pesticides. By adding values to self-descriptions, a blogger directs the understanding of his or her entries; if this guidance is challenged, the result can be lost readers. Accordingly, the values expressed are expected to conform to the values of those visiting the blog.

The blog communication pattern: This is characterised by communication frames of pleasure, enthusiasm, mutual agreement, and also hope (e.g., for better results). These blog networks have established a feel-good atmosphere, in which suggestions for improving sustainability and arguments for purchasing new, trendy plants meet with general approval. This feel-good atmosphere stands in stark contrast to the apocalyptic anxiety rhetoric of the news media's coverage of environmental issues. It is striking that comments almost always express agreement and often even admiration. The worst that can happen, apparently, is to receive no comments. This communication culture derives from the content: gardening as a mutual, pleasurable hobby. The blogs resemble lifestyle media in that they focus on personal pleasure and well-being (Graf 2011, 2012).

The general environmental morality of society: Communication involves morality, meaning what one ought to do in order to behave ecologically. Within the circles of garden bloggers, it has been considered common sense to prioritise sustainable gardening in communication, to work towards increasing biodiversity, to economise the use of natural resources, etc. For example, one can expect approval if one shows that one buys locally produced food or bee-friendly flowers. This may explain why communication about damage to the environment, for example by the use of chemicals, is almost entirely absent.

This mode of operation acts as a filter for selecting information from the non-human environment (e.g., one's own garden, nature, the weather) and the social environment (e.g., the economy, the media) in order to organise blog communication. Blogging is not so much about convincing people with different opinions as it is about coordinating the network of people who share similar interests and opinions. Bloggers and readers probably follow the blogs that share their values: If one is passionate about sustainable gardening and wishes to learn methods for doing it better, one may follow the blogs that are dedicated to this practice. If one is primarily passionate about garden design and garden renewal trends, one may follow blogs in that stream instead. Readers are unlikely to read, or get involved with, blogs that hold views opposed to their own.

References

Bauman, Zygmunt, *Consuming Life* (Cambridge: Polity, 2007).

Bonner, Frances, 'Digging for Difference: British and Australian Television Gardening Programmes', in *Exposing Lifestyle Television: The Big Reveal*, ed. by Gareth Palmer (Aldershot: Ashgate, 2008), pp. 25–38.

Bosch Studie, *The Virtual Art of Gardening. Bosch-Studie blickt Hobbygärtnern im Internet über die Schulter* (2011), http://linkfluence.com/de/2011/06/17/the-virtual-art-of-gardening-bosch-studie-blickt-hobbygartnern-im-internet-uber-die-schulter

Christensen, Christa L., 'Livsstil som tv-underholdning', *Mediekultur: Journal of Media and Communication Research*, 24(45) (2008), 23–36, http://dx.doi.org/10.7146/mediekultur.v24i45.513

Corbett, Julia, *Communicating Nature. How We Create and Understand Environmental Messages* (Washington: Island Press, 2006).

Foust, Christina R., and O'Shannon, William M., 'Revealing and Reframing Apocalyptic Tragedy in Global Warming Discourse', *Environmental Communication: A Journal of Nature and Culture*, 3(2) (2009), 151–167, http://dx.doi.org/10.1080/17524030902916624

Fuchs, Stephan, *Against Essentialism. A Theory of Culture and Society* (Cambridge, MA: Harvard University Press, 2001).

Global Garden Report. Husqvarna, Gardena (2010), http://corporate.husqvarna.com/files/Husqvarna_garden_report_2010_en.pdf

Graf, Heike, 'Recapturing Eden: Gardening Blogs as Ecological Communication Forums', Paper presented at the conference *Current Issues in European Cultural Studies*, organised by the Advanced Cultural Studies Institute of Sweden (ACSIS) in Norrköping, 15–17 June 2011. Conference Proceedings (Linköping: Linköping University Electronic Press, 2011), http://www.ep.liu.se/ecp_home/index.en.aspx?issue=062

—, 'Examining Garden Blogs as a Communication System', *International Journal of Communication*, 6 (2012), 2758–2779.

—, 'From Wasteland to Flower Bed: Ritual in the Website Communication of Urban Activist Gardeners', *Culture Unbound: Journal of Current Cultural Research*, 6(2) (2014), 451–471, http://dx.doi.org/10.3384/cu.2000.1525.146451 #sthash.9LFZ2BnA.dpuf

Gurak, Laura J., Antonijevic, Smiljana, Johnson, Laurie, Ratliff, Clancy and Reyman, Jessica, 'Into the Blogosphere: Rhetoric, Community, and Culture of Weblogs' (2004), http://conservancy.umn.edu/handle/11299/172840

Haider, Jutta, 'The Shaping of Environmental Information in Social Media: Affordances and Technologies of Self-Control', *Environmental Communication: A Journal of Nature and Culture*, 10(4) (2015), 473–491, http://dx.doi.org/10.10 80/17524032.2014.993416

Hellmann, Kai-Uwe, *Fetische des Konsums: Studien zur Soziologie der Marke* (Berlin: Springer-Verlag, 2011).

Lenhart, Amanda, *Bloggers: A Portrait of the Internet's New Storytellers* (Pew Internet & American Life Project, 2006), http://www.pewinternet.org/files/ old-media/Files/Reports/2006/PIP Bloggers Report July 19 2006.pdf.pdf

Lopez, Lori Kido, 'The Radical Act of "Mommy Blogging": Redefining Motherhood through the Blogosphere', *New Media & Society*, 11(5) (2009), 729–747, http://dx.doi.org/10.1177/1461444809105349

Lüders, Marika, Prøitz, Lin and Rasmussen, Terje, 'Emerging Personal Media Genres', *New Media & Society*, 12(6) (2010), 947–963, http://dx.doi. org/10.1177/1461444809352203

—, *Soziale Systeme. Grundriss einer allgemeinen Theorie* (Frankfurt am Main: Suhrkamp, 1987).

—, *Die Realität der Massenmedien* (Opladen: Westdeutscher Verlag, 1996).

—, *Ökologische Kommunikation. Kann die moderne Gesellschaft sich auf ökologische Gefährdungen einstellen?* (Wiesbaden: VS Verlag für Sozialwissenschaften, 2008).

—, *Introduction to Systems Theory* (Cambridge: Polity, 2013).

McKay, George, *Radical Gardening: Politics, Idealism & Rebellion in the Garden* (London: Frances Lincoln, 2011).

Merchant, Carolyn, *Reinventing Eden: The Fate of Nature in Western Culture* (Oxford: Routledge, 2013), http://dx.doi.org/10.4324/9780203079645

Milstein, Tema, 'Nature Identification: The Power of Pointing and Naming', *Environmental Communication: A Journal of Nature and Culture*, 5(1) (2011), 3–24, http://dx.doi.org/10.1080/17524032.2010.535836

Nadel-Klein, Jane, 'Gardening in Time: Happiness and Memory in American Horticulture', in *The Ethnographic Self as Resource: Writing Memory and Experience into Ethnography*, ed. by Peter Collins and Anselma Gallinat (New York: Berghahn Books, 2010), pp. 165–184.

Pole, Antoinette, *Blogging the Political: Politics and Participation in a Networked Society* (Oxford: Routledge, 2010).

Schmidt, Jan, *Weblogs. Eine kommunikationssoziologische Studie* (Konstanz: UVK Publishing, 2006).

Shannon, Claude E., and Weaver, Warren, *The Mathematical Theory of Communication* (Urbana: University of Illinois Press, 1949).

Siles, Ignacio, 'The Rise of Blogging: Articulation as a Dynamic of Technological Stabilization', *New Media & Society*, 14(5) (2012), 781–797, http://dx.doi. org/10.1177/1461444811425222

Smith, Antonia, 'The Farm Wife Mystery School: Women's Use of Social Media in the Contemporary North American Urban Homestead Movement', *Studies in the Education of Adults*, 47(2) (2015), 142–159.

Taekke, Jesper, 'Media Sociography on Weblogs', Paper presented at the Sixth Annual Media Ecology Association Convention (Fordham University, Lincoln Center Campus, New York City, 2005, June 22–26), http://pure. au.dk/portal/files/17826307/weblogs.pdf

Taylor, Lisa, 'It was Beautiful Before You Changed it All: Class, Taste and the Transformative Aesthetics of the Garden Lifestyle Media', in *Ordinary Lifestyles. Popular Media, Consumption and Taste*, eds. by David Bell and Joanne Hallows (Maidenhead: Open University Press, 2005), pp. 113–127.

Thomas, Lyn, '"Ecoreality": The Politics and Aesthetics of "Green" Television', in *Exposing Lifestyle Television. The Big Reveal*, ed. by Gareth Palmer (Aldershot: Ashgate, 2008), pp. 177–188.

Van Doorn, Niels, van Zoonen, Liesbet, and Wyatt, Sally, 'Writing from Experience Presentations of Gender Identity on Weblogs', *European Journal of Women's Studies*, 14(2) (2007), 143–158, http://dx.doi. org/10.1177/1350506807075819

Verdi, Laura, 'The Garden and The Scene of Power', *Space & Culture*, 7(4) (2004), 360–385, http://dx.doi.org/10.1177/1206331204266194

Blogs

Das wilde Gartenblog, http://www.das-wilde-gartenblog.de

Fundera Grönt, http://www.funderagront.blogspot.com

Günstig gärtnern, http://www.guenstiggaertnern.blogspot.com

Hannu På Kinnekulle, http://www.hannu-s.blogspot.com

Landet Krokus, http://www.landetkrokus.se

Lindas Trädgårdsblogg, http://www.lindastradgard.blogspot.com

Mauerblumen, http://www.mauerblumen.blogspot.com

Nervenruh, http://www.nervenruh.blogspot.com

Njut i Din Trädgård, http://www.czmastergarden.blogspot.com

Trädgårdstankar, http://www.tradgards-tankar.blogspot.com

Trädgårdstoken, http://www.tradgardstoken.se

Trädgårstankar comment, http://www.blogger.com/comment.g?blogID=246658
779628727907&postID=67269702330021335637

Wir Sind im Garten, http://www.hobby-garten-blog.de

Wurzels Garten, http://www.wurzerlsgarten.blogspot.com

6. The Militant Media of Neo-Nazi Environmentalism

Madeleine Hurd and Steffen Werther

The idea of an ecologist neo-Nazi seems, at first, ridiculous. Is one to imagine skinheads biking, in formation, bringing their milk-cartons to recycling centres? Well, no, not exactly: but many neo-Nazi parties have an environmentalist side to their party platforms. Neo-Nazi politicians espouse many standard environmentalist planks; neo-Nazi websites condemn pollution; neo-Nazi youth spend time cleaning parks. Indeed, environmentalism and militant xenophobia seem oddly compatible. In this chapter, we will look at how neo-Nazi websites and print media wed the slogans, symbols, visuals, and narratives of the radical patriot to those of the home-land-loving environmentalist, and how this combination results in a surprisingly coherent set of complementary media messages (or media 'frame').

We are interested in the symbols, slogans, narratives, and visuals used to package the combined environmentalist/right-wing extremist message. We are particularly interested in two emotional media frames. The first is the frame of fear and anger; the second, that of nostalgia and love. Fear concerns threats to the German people, and the need for militant action against its enemies. Nostalgia imbues neo-Nazi visions of what must be protected. Both frames are combined in a narrative of 'irreparability', effectively linking the visuals and narratives of militant xenophobia to biocentric environmentalism.

We are equally interested in how the neo-Nazi media seek to trigger environmentalist action. Their triggers range from suggestions

　　http://dx.doi.org/10.11647/OBP.0096.06

for everyday practices to political action and drawn-out descriptions of ritualised group performances. These promote a variety of reader roles: whether you are a concerned consumer, back-to-earth gardener, worried parent, animal-lover, or anti-globalisation activist, you can be included in the right-wing environmentalist coalition. The resultant actions are re-presented, with appropriate tone, narrative, and visuals, in the neo-Nazis' media. These narratives and visuals, together with the triggers themselves, help reinforce the environmentalist slant held, by those same media, such that it becomes integral to the central neo-Nazi message of racist xenophobia.

Our case history is the media of the National-Democratic Party of Germany (Nationaldemokratische Partei Deutschlands, or NPD), with an emphasis on the years 2010–2013. The NPD was, during these years — and despite its small size — preeminent on the German far right. One-time competitors had either declined into political insignificance (e.g., the so-called Republikaner) or been subsumed into the NPD (Deutsche Volksunion). Nor did Germany — in contrast to neighbouring countries such as Holland, Austria, Denmark, and Switzerland — produce a major right-wing populist party systematically willing to tap the vote potential of xenophobia. This, of course, has changed in subsequent years; but in the early 'teens, the NPD did command some ideological centrality.[1]

This German party — like extremists elsewhere — has had to tread a thin line between attracting loosely organised, violence-prone militants, and the more respectable voters from whom the pary gains a parliamentary presence. The NPD has, in fact, continued to acknowledge and collaborate (to some extent) with local, loosely organised hooligan forces such as Freie Kameradschaften and Freie

---

1   During 2013, the political constellation shifted somewhat. The far-right party Alternative für Deutschland (AfD) was founded as a protest party against German participation in the euro's financial politics. Between 2013 and 2015, the AfD mushroomed into a more general populist right-wing party. It has representatives in five German *Landtag*. It has, at the moment of writing, the support of around 10% of all German voters. This turn to the right has positioned the AfD as a direct competitor to the NPD, especially in Eastern Germany (conservative politicians have designated it 'NPD light'). The NPD has been able to maintain its own voter base, but has not grown — the AfD steals the additional voters it might have gained as sentiment hardens towards financial aid to Greece and the ongoing 'refugee crisis'.

Kräfte (*Verfassungsschutzbericht* 2012, 93). Nonetheless, the party has — like similar parties in other countries — increasingly moved towards parliamentary respectability. So far, its success has been modest. It did not garner more than 1.3%-1.5% of the vote in the 2009 and 2013 federal elections (around 560,000 individual votes), and has only around 6,000 formally registered members.

These poor returns disguise the party's substantial local presence, however. The NPD has gained around 350 mandates in county elections, receiving — twice running — the 5% of votes in Mecklenburg-Vorpommern and Sachsen needed to take a place in the *Landtag*. On the communal level, it can be a factor indeed. In some communities, the NPD may rely on a steady 20% of the votes (Brandstetter 2012, 9). At this level, the actions of militants can be felt — in threats of vandalism and arson. After all, direct-action militants and voters go together: as Karl Richter put it in 2011, they make up 'two edges of the same sword, both fighting for the *Volk*' in the movement of 'national resistance' (*Verfassungsschutzbericht* 2011, 89).

Fig. 6.1 Screenshot of NPD folder, 'Our program: a decent Heimat as the foundation of our *Volkstums*'. Source: NPD homepage; http://www.npd.de/inhalte/daten/dateiablage/ThemenHeimat_2010.pdf

The face-to-face world of direct action thus remains an important element in NPD appeal and recruitment. If, on the one hand, the party pays a price for refusing to cut its ties to the street activists — it is, for instance, adversely affected by police exposure of the activities of the neo-Nazi terrorist group 'Nationalsozialistischer Untergrund' (NSU) — it has, on the other, the continued appeal of intense camaraderie, either in street actions or in nationalist ceremonies and marches. Triggers for and reports on such camaraderie are packaged into party media, forming a managed web of communicative relationships. The emotions, visuals, and rituals of these group performances (often presented as image events) are, we argue, key in linking the party's politics to environmentalism.

NPD Media: Party Websites

The party's message is conveyed via a variety of networked forums, including party websites, blogs, Twitter, YouTube videos, magazines, fanzines, and leaflets. There are, moreover, street media: demonstrations, flags, speeches, songs, clothing, tattoos, car-and-lamppost stickers, all of which contribute strong visuals and slogans to the party's political, social, and traditional media. We will concentrate on the NPD websites, with special attention to how the party's environmentalist message is networked both with its sub-organisations' sites and with an openly pro-NPD environmentalist magazine. Our research covers, roughly, the years between 2010 and 2013.

What metaphors, symbols, and rhetoric are used to promote the emotional frames (fear, nostalgia) and narratives (heroic epic, irreparability) that allow the seemingly effortless wedding of far-right extremism and environmentalism? How are these gendered; what kinds of time-spaces are envisioned? What types of performances are encouraged — and how are performance narratives fed back into the websites, so as to strengthen the message?

The NPD party's national and 'Landes' websites (npd.de, npd-bayern. de, npd.mv.de, etc.) provide visuals and text in the service of symbols, slogans, and narratives. They are networked with other media; and there are a multitude of invitations to reader action ('triggers'): write messages or ask questions, order a product or donate money, learn more about or join a group. The reader chooses between different banner headlines (each with an evocative image), and clicks to read party news, history, and activities, as well as national and international news blurbs. A search engine simplifies things for those seeking information on any one issue or the most recent party and activist activities.

In 2013, the party's websites were dominated by the NPD's electioneering slogans, short pieces on its political-social crusades, descriptions of and suggestions for street and political action against various threats, as well as the faces, deeds, and words of its political leaders. Images invited readers to respond to slogans and click on further options: *Aktuelles, Partei, aktiv werden* [news, party, become active]. Under *Partei* — illustrated by a smiling blue-eyed blonde girl against flowers, a favourite NPD symbol (http://npd.de/themen/) — the reader could pick through the party's premises, choosing, e.g., 'Often Asked' with answers to questions such as 'Is the NPD Hostile to Foreigners?', 'Why Does the NPD Oppose the Multi-Cultural Society?' and 'Is the NPD Anti-Semitic? Surely It Is Permissible to Criticise Jews Too' (npd.de/oftgefragt/).

Emotions

Most texts are brisk and angry in tone. The exception is when it comes to descriptions of what is at risk: then, texts become nostalgic and lyrical. On the whole, however, focus is on the party, portrayed as a never-surrendering vanguard. The party leads the battle against the *Volk*'s enemies: international elites, the majority parties, the mainstream media.

An epic narrative (available through a click on 'History') constitutes the party's autobiography. Founded in 1964, the NPD presents itself as waging an unswerving battle against the unremitting foes of 'the German people'. It is the 'only true resistance movement'. The party will never cease to address burning issues — 'no matter how the bankrupt [mainstream] parties shift and turn' — for every day is a 'day lost to our *Volk* and its life-interests'. '[O]ur determination' to 'take over the leadership of Germany' remains 'unbroken' (http://npd.de/geschichte/). There is a great sense of urgency throughout; it is a matter of war against inhuman enemies. These are, in their turn, usually spoken of with deep contempt, if not with leaden 'humour' in contrast to the hyper-masculinist, courageous *Kameradschaft* [cameradie] of national heroes.

Standard metaphors, well-known to scholars of Nazi rhetoric, paint the war in simple colours. There is the innocent German *Volk* — unfortunately, a favourite 'host' for 'nomadic' 'parasites', its purity threatened by 'corruption' and 'contamination'. The threat comes from groups alien to the *Volk* (e.g., 'Nomadentum' — in older parlance, 'Judentum'; today, the 'US in collaboration with the EU'). Allowed into the *Volk*'s Germany, through the 'back-door' by the 'profit-hungry machinations' of 'a few tens of thousands of profiteers', the 'internationalist corrupters of the *Volk*' collaborate with domestic 'do-gooders, liberals, and internationalists' to destroy the foundations for *Volk* existence. These are not people as much as abstractions or, perhaps, vermin: 'The collected enemies of our *Volk* and country have been gnawing away at the NPD for nigh-on fifty years'.

The result: the German people, characterised by 'honour, history and pride', are at terrible risk. Prevented from 'knowing their own traditions, singing their own songs, living according to their own habits and customs, saving their *Heimat* for their children, preventing the immigration of foreigners' (note how the last is a precondition for the *Volk*'s otherwise innocuous actions), they are 'threatened with extinction'. But 'every *Volk* has a right to survival'; 'we will never allow [its destruction]' (see npd.bayern: *Völkerschützer*; npd.de/geschichte; https://www.facebook.com/npd.de; https://nsantispe.wordpress.com).

The websites allow no room for comments and discussion (this would invite disruption from organisations such as Antifaschistische Aktion). Nonetheless, the general tone implicitly, and many texts explicitly, urges readers to get involved. There are 'want to contribute?' and 'join us!' buttons. Links encourage readers to learn about and participate in the party's women and youth movements. Local websites give details of planned events, demonstrations, music festivals, and the like. One can, moreover, visit (and probably join) their Facebook page and follow their Twitter account. A few clicks lead the reader, finally, to pages advertising downloadable pamphlets ('Work With Us. Change Things. Act.'), leaflets and posters, as well as the paraphernalia of street communication: stickers, T-shirts, emblems, buttons, caps, all imprinted with the party logo or various right-wing symbols (the Iron Cross, the

German Eagle, an outline of 'the stolen *Heimat*'; see npd-materialdienst. de).

The sites are heavily visual. Images evoke either nostalgia and affection (the *Volk* and the *Heimat* to be protected), or fear and hate (the enemy). The sites' images alternate, accordingly, between classic German statues, little blonde girls, snow-covered pine branches with Christmas lights, picturesque townscapes, families holding hands in a field, *and* dark silhouettes of knife-wielding foreigners, cows with their throats bloodily cut, looming burka-clad figures, EU skyscrapers, the state tax office. The former images dominate in presentations of party ideology and doings; the latter, in news of the world at large.

Fig. 6.2 Screenshot of NPD's Facebook page, 'Animal protection is protection of the Heimat! Vote for the NPD on September 22!' Campaign poster for the 2013 German federal elections. Source: NPD Facebook page, http://www.facebook.com/npd.de/photos/ pb.268232929583.-2207520000.1461139625./10151722063984584/?type=3&theater

That world, indeed, seems to be in a state of war. The sites' media logic leads their controllers to select items that reinforce the master narrative that informs the whole: the *Volk* under attack. In 2011, to take one example, the news on the NPD Bavaria website (arranged under various banner icons) was dominated by the threats posed by profit mongering, internationalism, immigrants, and foreign culture. The banner choice of *Heimat* gives one, accordingly, an 'Open Letter' protesting housing for asylum-seekers and an exposé of the Sochi Winter Olympics profit mongering. An article entitled 'Turkish flags over Würzburg' warns that

Turkish 'guest workers' have arrived in Germany not because Germany needs workers, but because NATO and the US have forced Germany to accept the surplus people of an overpopulated Turkey. An image of a placidly happy cow precedes a blurb protesting the low prices paid by (good) German dairy farmers; a bloody, dying cow illustrates Turkish 'cruelty to animals' (npd.bayern: Meldungen 2011).

This media logic — framing the narrative of battle, the emotion of fear and anger, protecting the loved family and country from threat — remains constant over the years. In November/December 2013, homepage headlines included 'Stop, At Long Last, the Import of Criminal Foreigners' (with a picture of a knife-holding hand against a black-clad torso); 'Against the Sell-Out Of Citizenship and the Liquidation of the German People!'; and 'Asylum-Seekers Can Bring Serious Illnesses to Germany' (npd.de: Meldungen Nov/Dec 2013).

At the time of writing (6 January 2016), the website npd.de provides a running slide-show: the stereotypical little blonde girl, profiled against a bed of Rudbeckia ('Work, Family, *Heimat*, Our Program for Germany'); an open, people-filled boat on a tidal wave, with a no-entry sign superimposed over a map of Europe ('The Boat is Full — Stop the Deluge of Asylum-Seekers'); and a bronze statue of a sword-wielding warrior ('The NPD Defends Itself!'). Four editorials are presented: one on 'foreigners' massive assaults in Köln, Hamburg and Stuttgart' proving that 'mass immigration' is a 'threat'; the second, protesting that the Bundeswehr, or armed forces, must be used against threats inside Germany; the third, calling for 'a state of law instead of integration insanity'; and the fourth, maintaining that the 'majority of Germans see immigration as no enrichment' — rather, 'mass immigration' is condemned as bringing only 'financial burdens, growing organised criminality and a risk of Islamist attacks hitherto unknown to Germany'. The four 'short notices' on the side of the page include, in the same tone, the promise of 'a list of the attempted and successful homicides by asylum-seekers in Saxony alone' and the exhortation to 'protect our women, our constitutional rights, and our German *Heimat* against foreign criminals' (npd.de: Meldungen Dec 2015–Jan 2016).

The NPD presents itself as engaged in nationalist struggle, awakened to danger from invading foreigners and actively fighting — in the teeth of the establishment — these enemies of the German people. The *Volk* to be protected is presented, in turn, less in words than in saccharine images: an agrarian or small-town idyll of happy, healthy families (with a strong emphasis on small blonde girls). The dark threats to this idyll, as shown by the news items and their accompanying images, give the websites an emotional frame that combines nostalgia for a (familial, feminine) world of harmony, security, and beauty with fear, anger, and urgency (adult, masculine, soldierly).

The narrative structure that carries these emotional frames conforms to Robert Cox's use of the term 'irreparable' as a narrative descriptor (2013, 384–385). Media using this narrative call on readers to act now, urgently, immediately because the 'irreparable' is just around the corner. Otherwise, they risk the destruction of the most valuable thing in the world, the precondition for their existence. It is already weak, polluted, threatened; soon it will be too late; once destroyed, it — and they — will be lost forever. Cox cites this narrative appeal as common within environmentalist media forums. As NPD websites prove, it has equal resonance for the narratives, metaphors, and emotions that inform the neo-Nazis' media logic. It should come as no surprise, then, that the neo-Nazi narrative can incorporate environmentalism. Let us now turn to how the two narratives of 'irreparability' are merged.

The NPD and the Environment

First, let us establish that environment *was* a NPD media concern. The npd.de website's 'party program' provided information on the party's stance on a number of issues. Among the more standard matters, such as 'Society: Living in Germany, Justly and Economically' and 'Family: Children and Families Are Our Future', there appears 'The Environment: Protect Our Living Space!'

When one clicks, one is presented with an image of what seems to be a primeval German forest. An introductory text frames the political measures proposed. These are manifold. The state must intervene against 'unbounded economic growth', promote local production, end cheap-wage food imports, stop chemical waste dumping, and protect water supplies. The NPD opposes any import of genetically modified foods. Agriculture is to be protected. Animal transports are to be minimised, and laws passed that increase the 'punishment of those who torture animals'. 'Religiously motivated methods of butchering such as *Schächten* [halal slaughter] are to be criminalised'. To round it off, 'Perverse practices of sodomy are to be forbidden and punished as severely as possible' (npd.de/thema/umwelt).

Fig. 6.3 Screenshot of NPD homepage, 'Environment: Protect our *Lebensraum*'.
Source: http://www.npd.de/thema/umwelt

The party's Bavarian affiliate likewise posts a separate party plank on the environment. It wishes to encourage alternative sources of energy; regional self-sufficiency; a ban on atomic energy; rebuilding towns on a human, familial scale; the promotion of ecological agriculture and businesses; and strong legal enforcement of resource husbandry and environmental protection. 'Ethical principles' must come before economic growth: 'Humans and nature are not economic goods!' (npd. bayern: Eine intakte Natur).

These measures fit, in fact, within the frame proposed by the plank's introductory text. It runs as follows:

> NPD endorses a comprehensive protection of our *Heimat* as living space for humans and animals. We refuse to countenance the profit-maximising degradation of space, resources, and living beings, in accordance with our holistic understanding of natural interdependence and cooperation and because of our responsibility for the future. (npd.de/thema/umwelt)

Ecologically, this is a fairly radical statement. Most parties go no further than (the fairly anthropocentric) planks of sustainability and preservation. Few ecocritics would find fault with a 'holistic understanding of natural interdependence' in a 'living space for humans and animals'. Most would share the hostility to 'the profit-maximising degradation of space, resources, and living beings'. Similarly, ecocritics might agree with particular statements in defence of local production and knowledge:

> Our farmers must not become defenceless victims of banks, EU-bureaucrats, and international seed and fertiliser distributors [...] The protection of the natural foundations of life is, in our opinion, of the highest priority. We do not accept the subordination of the active protection of nature to unbounded economic growth. (npd.de/thema/umwelt)

We have met these enemies before — internationalists, capitalists, the EU. The goods to be protected — traditional, place-bound, harmonious — are also familiar. The leaflet 'The Right to Heimat' (offered for download on the same website) makes things doubly clear. *Heimat* is the key concept. A people's right to its *Heimat*, the territory which nourishes it and to which it is tied by history and tradition, is the 'most important collective human right'. Within certain borders, it seems, people and nature co-evolved, producing a unique *Volk*, culture, and landscape. '*Volkstum* and culture are essential foundations of human worth [...] because of this, resident groups have made the *Heimat* an object of protection for centuries'. The pamphlet's cover presents the imagined idyll: an old stone house in green, garden-like countryside. But this idyllic *Heimat* of 'all European peoples' has its enemies:

> cultural imperialism, the destruction of the environment, and globalisation [cause...] the systematic destruction of our identity and consciousness of our *Heimat*. Our roots are replaced by mere consumption. The destruction of the environment, the result of years of rapacity on the part of global big capital, eliminates the prerequisites for our existence. (npd.de: Recht auf *Heimat*)

A *Volk*, it seems, is defined by its culture, which has evolved, historically, in dialectic with its territory: the result is the *Heimat*. 'Therefore and fundamentally', *The Right to Heimat* pamphlet continues, 'environmental protection can never be divided from cultural evolution' (ibid.). For this reason, the Bavarian website explains, 'unbounded economic growth, overambitious, overgrown industrial projects, the industrialisation of agriculture, the urbanisation of villages' are to be condemned: they lead to the 'destruction of traditional links and cultures'. Humans, when 'uprooted from their environment', are deprived of identity (npd. bayern: Eine intakte Natur). A *Heimat*'s territory, culture, and people are one; 'our' identity cannot exist without all three. There is no division, it seems, between culture and nature. If one's *Heimat* is despoiled, the website goes on to explain, the *Volk* is threatened in 'its very substance' (ibid.). Again, ecocritics would agree with much of this reasoning — if not the conclusions.

The far right's belief that different peoples are defined by their historical interaction with specific landscapes and climates has its roots, as Jonathan Olsen (1990) has shown, in a European-wide neo-Romantic ideology. Popularised in the nineteenth century, and reinforced in the twentieth, by pseudo-scientific biological determinism, it holds that peoples are partly determined by their specific natural milieu, as expressed in their culture, language, and history. This (as Olsen puts it) means believing that all people are 'the expression of an "eco-niche", the places, nations, and cultures to which they naturally belong'. Each *Volk* is held to be unique — and 'the most natural thing on earth' (Olsen 1990, 6; see also Ditt 2001; Sharma 2012).

Or, to paraphrase Olsen's argument, the far-right myth holds that the German people have developed both biomass and culture in fundamental interaction with the land and animals surrounding them. This is the *Heimat* that must be protected. But neo-Nazis take the reasoning in an unpleasant direction. If Germans are to survive, they must protect German nature and land against non-German immigrants. Such immigrants, as the product of altogether other natural systems, are necessarily alien to German nature and culture. They can only cause harm. Indeed, their need to leave their original *Heimat* shows how they have already ruined their own land. But worse still, of course, are those with no *Heimat* at all. Here we have, e.g., the international capitalists. Anchored, according to some NPD texts, in the 'East Coast of the US', they shade into the spectre of international Jewry.

In their critique of international capitalism, we again find strains faintly reminiscent of left-wing ecocriticism. Militant ecology, reborn in the 1970s, included left- and right-wing streams. Both condemned imperialism and international capitalism, with a special focus on their destruction of local environments. Indeed, left and right environmentalism share enemies. Ecological activism, Olsen argues, appeals to humans' identity-affirming connection to the immediate natural world. Consequently, many environmentalists warn — again, in Olsen's words — against the 'homogenizing globalism that turns place into space and home into nowhere in particular' (1990, 5). This emotional attachment and fear of loss are linked as easily to the right as to the left. For the former, it becomes an argument for territorial exclusiveness. We must defend our (fragile and essential) place — culture, nature, and people — from invaders and despoilers. Or according to the NPD's environmentalist slogan: 'Protection of the environment is protection of the *Heimat*'. For, as the Bavarian NPD website puts it in its party program, 'An Intact Nature is the Foundation of Our Future':

> National politics is environmental politics. The lack of ecologically responsible politics threatens every *Volk* in its substance. Economic interests must come second to the protection of nature. The human is part of nature. Nature, therefore, is not simply the '*Umwelt*' of humans, their physical space, but also the *Mitwelt*, their cultural environment (npd.bayern: Eine intakte Natur).

The enemies of this natural *Mitwelt*, aided by a *Heimat*-denying establishment, are themselves outside. It is outdoors that alien biomass, polluting and weakening the combined human-nature world, attacks: immigrants and their children, waste-dumpers, the international transport of food, the import of genetically modified crops, invasive species, foreign plants, trash and littering, cruelty to and perverse sexual actions with animals. It's a matter of biomass misplaced: too little of the good, too much of the alien. (Indeed, the 2013 NPD website advertises condoms labelled 'For Foreigners' as a means of averting 'demographic catastrophe'; npd.de: Kondome). Let us look at some details of how all these aspects are packaged into a single media message.

The Neo-Nazi World of *Umwelt & Aktiv*

Here, we turn to the quarterly pro-NPD environmentalist periodical *Umwelt & Aktiv* [Environment & Active]. This Magazine for Holistic Thinking: Environmental Protection, Animal Protection, Protection of the Heimat is available (along with the anti-foreigner condoms) on the npd.de web-page. If one clicks on the link, reads the extensively informational website, and orders the magazine, one receives about 35 pages of folksy, glossy, colourful 'environmentalist' news and features. *Umwelt & Aktiv* has no advertisers; it has been active for about ten years. As German journalists and anti-fascist groups have repeatedly pointed out, it is run and written by more or less openly committed NPD members (Pfaffinger 2014; Najoks 2008; Valjent 2012: recherche-nord.com 2014, ndr.de 2013).

The magazine website presents a 'Letter of Welcome' to visitors and subscribers, which immediately makes the nature-territory-culture-*Volk* connection.

> The protection of nature begins at home, in the native (*heimischen*) woods, mountains, lakes, and beaches — in short, the *Heimat*. And thereto belongs also the protection of culture as the natural bearer of local environmental and animal protection, free from commercial imperatives [...] We must think of ourselves, our children, and our country! (*U&A*.de: Wir über uns)

How is this message made flesh? Let us suppose ourselves to have ordered a fourth-quarter issue (2011). Here we find our familiar enemies, in articles on African and Indian small farmers combating international seed monopolies; in condemnations of industrial animal farming (accompanied by a picture of dead, bloody hen); and, under 'Protection of the *Heimat*', an exposé of the foreign purchase of German agricultural land (a giant hand embossed with a dollar sign hovering over a field). Other threats to German biomass are also on the move: there is a condemnation of 'bad food' (a hamburger impaled by American and EU flags), while German biomass itself is self-imploding — as an article blaming Germany's declining birth-rate on the mainstream media's celebration of career-minded women makes clear. Finally, there is the nostalgic counter-frame, that of the (threatened) beloved: a celebration of homeopathic medicines (juxtaposing herbs to needles), the picture of a mother nursing her child that illustrates the career-women article, and visually-rich articles and poems on the significance of the time-honoured, essentially German celebration of Advent and 'Jul' (*U&A* 2011, 4).

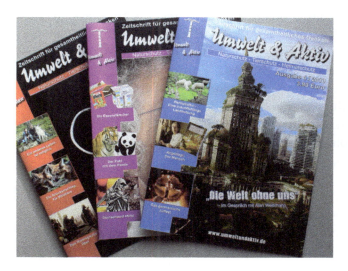

Fig. 6.4 Sample issues of *Umwelt & Aktiv*. Photo: Steffen Werther.

These three themes — the enemy, the urgency, the beloved — convene under the combined right-wing/environmentalist narrative of irreparability. Environmentalism and right-wing ideology are usually intermixed. The standard anti-globalisation, pro-environment information is given a special slant: the need to protect German (and European) biomass. Why, asks one article, are '800 million Africans' leaving their own countries? The reason is that they are driven out by the plundering of multinationals and their own population explosions. Why are they 'waiting to go to Europe?' Because of that continent's population 'vacuum'. Can anyone believe, the writer asks, that border guards and walls will prevent Europe from being 'filled by immigrants'? The place of Africans, the writer concludes snidely, 'is in African wars of liberation, not in the social service and anti-discrimination bureaus of Europe' (*U&A* 2011, 2).

Indeed, all alien bodies — *and* their alien culture and practices — should be kept at bay. Otherwise, the essential link between people and nature will be at risk. For what is it besides the 'soulless *multi-kulti* society' that weakens Germans' relationship to nature — that nature which is the 'power resource for the German people and the spring of *Volk* health'?

Volk and nature should always be linked. Conversely, 'nationalism and the battle to maintain *Völker* are nothing more than the broadening of the idea of protecting nature to include humans'. For are not peoples 'a creation of nature'? And do not they, as a people, also deserve protection against extinction? But the German people will not survive a transmutation into 'identity-less coffee-brown mixtures, a collection of consumers', lacking sentiment for the 'fatherland' — which is, in turn, 'indissoluble from love of nature, tradition, *Heimat*, and family' (*U&A* 2010, 2).

There is no division between humans and nature here: the Germans' communal soul is part and parcel of the German environment. The converse is true as well: the biomass of the German environment must be protected, on behalf of the German soul. Foreigners must be kept doubly at bay. 'Now they are also plundering the woods'. Once, this Mecklenburg-Vorpommern NPD homepage article reads, 'before Germany became so colourful and international', gathering mushrooms had been a pleasant, relaxing past-time. Today, bands of Eastern Europeans are 'swarming' in search of mushrooms, picking the land bare, and destroying the woods. When a forester tried to stop them, he was first threatened at knife-point; then they tried to run him over. So far, this has been an isolated occurrence — perhaps; but 'Poland is nearby and the media lies' (npd.de: Pilze).

Like the NPD website, *Umwelt & Aktiv* is also concerned with the suffering that foreigners cause (German) animals. The culprits are, predictably, both commercial, industrial husbandry practices (the dead hen described above) and immigrants. Much ink is spilled denouncing kosher and halal slaughtering — foreign biomass (people) attacking German biomass (animals). Jewish and Muslim immigrants bring 'in their baggage a type of animal-torture as yet unknown to us', in contravention to 'the norms that obtain here'. Those who tolerate this torture of animals then, the author concludes with heavy-handed sarcasm, give 'an outraged howl, when Orientalist politico-terrorists cut, not the throats of sheep and cows, but of Western hostages' (*U&A* 2011, 1).

From humans to domestic animals, and thence to the rest of German nature. There are invasive fish, insect, and plant species as well. An article entitled 'Invasion from Asia' details the 'cannibalistic' and rapidly reproducing Asiatic ladybugs (juxtaposed to the German ladybug, the object of affectionate attention). The article 'Animal Immigrants' denounces an alien crayfish. Indeed, 'animals with migration background are on the increase' (*U&A* 2011, 2; 2010, 4).

And then there is the alien biomass that will be eaten by Germans (the EU-American hamburger is a typical example). 'Clone-Meat on German Plates' tells of one of many unwanted American biomass invasions: the invasion through genetically modified plants (*U&A* 2011, 2). *Umwelt & Aktiv* joins NPD Party websites in repeatedly attacking the spread of (American-sponsored) genetically modified crops. In the vividly illustrated 'The Dialogue Between Two Seeds, Geni and Normi', the latter weeps over 'an evil plan for immeasurable profits', hatched by the multinational American concern Monsanto, which plans, efficiently and secretly, to 'bring death and illness to humans' (*U&A* 2011, 1).

What would German biomass look like, then, if left in peace? The nostalgic counter-ideal is, predictably enough, that of the doughty, self-supporting small farmer. Here, indeed, the story suddenly broadens to mythic proportions, stretching back into the ur-History of the German people.

Ten thousand years ago, according to one *Umwelt & Aktiv* writer, the North European farmer cared for and nurtured 'his "Garden of Eden" in accordance with nature-derived understanding [*natürlichen Verstand*] — the opposite of the abstract, world-foreign intellect' (*U&A* 2011, 4). Indeed, as a website contributor explains, there was once an 'ancient European, "Nordic" culture', pagan, pure, and pro-environment, a culture that survived all subsequent immigration (*U&A*.de 2013: *Heimatschutz*). In the 'old pagan faith', another magazine author explains, 'scarcely a natural phenomenon existed which was not honoured as godlike'. There was a pantheistic idea of the 'souls intrinsic to all living creatures, the godliness of every living being' (*U&A* 2011, 4). The great perversion came with the 'Christianisation of the Germanic peoples'. Old beliefs were suppressed — including the 'deep and gripping love of nature', rooted in the 'Germanic soul', but missing altogether in the Bible (*U&A* 2009, 2). And today? We are in a 'capitalistic and atomised world that has to do only with profit maximising'. The brutal power of 'global concerns' leads to a psychologically impoverished 'consumption ideology' — 'the era of the total rule of money'. 'Synthetically homogenised space', in the opinion of another writer, 'is replacing what were, once, *stammesgeschichtlich* [historical-tribal] communities' (*U&A* 2010, 2; 2011, 2). Again, ecocritical tropes and narratives are meshed, unpleasantly, with those of militant nationalism.

Nature-Oriented Action: A Cure for National Ills

What are the neo-Nazi solutions? *Umwelt & Aktiv* does not mention the NPD (although the Party's environmentalist policies are, at one point, reproduced in full). But both party and *Umwelt & Aktiv* websites and publications provide plenty of recommendations for pro-nature action. *Umwelt & Aktiv* writers, in particular, direct their appeals to those mainstays of German environmentalism: the rediscovery and maintenance of the German's age-old interrelationship with and participation in nature.

This is done by recommending action on three levels. The first can be called everyday — a return to the practices of our ancestors. Here, *Umwelt & Aktiv* gives many cosy recommendations. There are ancient herbal medicines (as used by 'Wotan, as magical medicine'), 'aromatherapy' (associated in 'all old cultures' with 'godliness, purity, strength, and power'), bee-keeping, preserving fruit, and gardening. Then there is a second level, that of maintaining a pro-nature family culture. This will be triggered (the authors hope) by, for instance, articles on how to teach children to sing poems celebrating spring (*U&A* 2011, 1; 2011, 2; 2010, 2).

Both sets of practices, it will be noted, are heavily gendered: environmentalist racism, it seems, is one way of connecting women to what is otherwise a heavily masculinised movement. By the same token, emphasis on environmentalist everyday practices reinforces the feminine nature of the nostalgic and beloved, the wife-and-child home: the *Heimat*, which the male soldier protects against intrusion (here, evidently, the soldier stands for NPD activists; for more on the gendered nature of the *Heimat*, see Ecker 2002).

Much triggering, however, is directed to a third level of engagement: efforts to encourage groups, even communities, to join together in re-treading the paths of their ancestors. If we are to return, one writer urges, to the 'way of thinking' rooted 'in the Germanic', which respected and loved eagles, horses, deer, 'old trees and blooming bushes', we must hold fast to 'traditions and inherited values'. These are, it transpires, uniquely German, pre-Christian, and pro-environment (*U&A* 2009, 2). We should, for instance — as an article on solar energy puts it — revive solstice celebrations of 'Mother sun', the 'first god of life'. To be sure, state-sponsored festivals for the 'religious honouring of the sun' did occur under National Socialism; but since then, the alienation from nature inherent in industrialised farming has meant the steady demotion of the sun as a holy object. But perhaps the turn towards solar energy will bring back the old ways? (*U&A* 2011, 1).

The implications of reviving old group rituals are far-reaching: only by re-establishing the relationship between nature and humans can the German people be saved. 'The [tradition of the] April joke is dying out', complains one *Umwelt & Aktiv* writer: 'our regional dialects and customs are dying out, animal and plant species are dying out'. The '*Mischgesellschaft* [mixed society] caused by alien-ethnic immigration' has caused a 'loss of the way-of-life, of *Volkstum* and culture'. The threat of loss is dire: 'the German people is headed for extinction'.

> Perhaps still in small towns and villages, the May Pole is still raised [...] but is one really still greeting the beautiful, life-giving season of the sun? [...] who tends the family grave [...] who still knows by name the trees, flowers, and animals, growing at the roadside and in the woods? [...] all that which our people have made and that concerns them is almost totally suppressed. (*U&A* 2011, 3)

One solution to this looming problem seems to be extensive descriptions of how readers can enact 'traditional German' festivals. Here, the articles draw on highly charged, tradition-laden icons, framed in a ritualistic, solemn, and soothing narrative: that of liturgy and, hence, redemption. A pagan version of Christmas is, understandably, a favourite. The author of 'Christmas: Then, Today, and Tomorrow' tells us that 'Christmas is something special for us Germans', for 'most Christmas customs have Germanic roots'. These customs 'bring us people together and let us experience that we are part of a community' (*U&A* 2011, 4). 'The Germanic Jul-Festival' (which adds a, presumably pagan, burning circle of wood to the usual icons of snow-covered pines, candles, and nuts) goes further, giving step-by-step instructions on how to recreate the authentic pagan ritual. It presents itself as a paean of 'praise to nature' (*U&A* 2010, 4). The article is followed by a Viking-esque poem: 'Fall storms roar', but 'No weather-storm is too hard for us / we are of Nordland's *Art!*' (ibid.). Finally, the link between winter solstice and warrior ancestors is brought out on the magazine's back cover, where a German soldier and a lit candle illustrate the text 'Once a year, in the holy night / the dead warriors leave off their guard [...] We die for you, because we believe in Germany' (ibid.). The (familial) idyll nourishes (masculinist) activist militancy; the militants are needed to fight the idyll's enemies.

Local NPD websites also urge people to practice what they term 'culture-bearing' seasonal community traditions (that is, traditions that strengthen and uphold German culture). Besides giving instructions on how to conduct 'traditional' festivals, they publish lengthy reports on actual celebrations. Such reports are integral to triggering the local demonstrations, festivals, excursions, and hikes, the face-to-face encounters which make up an essential part of any social movement. Indeed, one finds a surprisingly rich set of narratives of everyday environmentalist and nature-oriented praxis. Let us turn to this last aspect of neo-Nazi environmentalist media: the interplay between media that seek to trigger nature-human festivals, and the subsequent presentation of these performances in that same media. How do this interplay affect the emotions and narratives that make up the eco-Nazi media frame?

Women, Youth, and Germanic Nature: From *Umwelt* to *Aktion*

The national NPD homepage is a bit too lofty to tell of local organisational doings, but local and sub-organisation websites give them a lot of space. There are political demonstrations; there is the annual commemorative event. Many events are meant to project the Party as a manly fighting organisation — mourning the deaths of martyrs, celebrating the founding of the party, meeting to drink beer and listen to speeches, the great music festivals, the convivial party-member outings to a war memorial or historic site. But many activities are seasonal and directly connected to nature. Let us look at several such activities, as reported on the two sub-organisation websites given prominence on the NPD's homepage: the Ring Nationaler Frauen (National Women Group, hereafter Ring) and the Junge Nationaldemokraten (National-Democratic Youth). These will, we hope, give an idea of how neo-Nazi media trigger actions — and reports on actions — that reinforce both their two central emotional frames and their overriding 'irreparable' narrative.

The Ring, although many years old, is not large; indeed, the 2012 Report by the Federal Agency for Internal Security put it at 100-odd members (*Verfassungschutzbericht* 2012, 103). Its main website (http://www.ring-nationaler-frauen-deutschland.de) is, judging from the entries, kept alive by female NPD representatives. Like the NPD's website, the Ring's is concerned with the doings of the party, political news, and organisation events. In accordance with the neo-Nazis' conservative gender norms, their website gives food, culture, customs, and traditions a first-place ranking. It is here that nature figures most prominently.

'Defence of the environment is defence of the *Heimat*', the NPD program maintains — and, predictably, neo-Nazi women have a role here. The Ring website posts invitations to, and lengthy reports on, group celebrations of German nature. A brief, 2014 dip into the website provides, for instance, an account of a 'Thüringer Advents-Aktion', where Ring members gave out home-made cookies and propaganda to passing women (whose eyes supposedly glowed with gratitude), as well as information on the ancient pagan roots of the St. Martin's Day celebration. There are also longer narratives, detailing members' doings, such as the Ring's 'Visit to native orchids' in the Schwäbische Alb. A 'whole meadow [...] full of different herbs' provides 'an impressive experience' of the 'well-known plants of our *Heimat*'. Finally, after enjoying the herbs (pictures are included) and the 'stupendous view of the Alb and the Hohenzollern Fortress', the women had some ice cream — 'after our time in the sun, a wonderful refreshment'. The harmonious, secure, child-like pleasures of traditional German nature-culture are thus offered (Ring.de: Advent; Orchid).

But the writers for this website want us, above all, to celebrate seasonal festivals, such as '"Mariae Himmelfahrt" and the Sprig of Herbs' and 'The Summer Solstice' (found under the *Customs and Culture* banner button). The roots of such festivals, we are repeatedly reminded, lie in purely Germanic culture. A piece on 'Carnival-Time', for instance, emphasises that the celebration long antedates Christianity; doubting readers are referred to Swedish stone inscriptions. Such practices, the writer explains, re-enact the fight between winter and summer, re-awakening sleeping nature and bidding it be fruitful. 'The winter is conquered, nature is woken' — and we are encouraged to participate in these rites of spring (Ring.de: Brauchtum; Mariae; Sommer; Fasching).

And then there are the harvest festivals, predictably paying homage to the threatened German farmer. 'The original harvest-festival customs, which have their roots in pagan history', consist, in fact, of 'the farmer's thanks for the successful harvest' as well as 'the people's thanks to the farmer'. This custom should be especially revered today, when foreign imports threaten 'our own sound *Bauerntum* [peasantry]' and people with 'the poisons in industrially produced food sources' and 'genentically manipulated agricultural products'. What is worse, the Germanic festival has been supplanted by Halloween, an American custom 'forced through by great commercial concerns' and the mainstream media (Ring.de: Herbst).

This trigger to action is complemented by a narrative of the Ring's proper celebration of the annual 'Harvest Thanks Festival' — 'already a tradition' (Ring.de: Erntedankfeier). The reader is provided with a ritualised narrative of happy, enthusiastic celebrants sharing food, songs ('Of Autumn'), and poetry in order to give thanks to farmers. The audience 'listened eagerly' to speeches on the value of the family, the avoidance of pesticides, and the profitibility of ecological vegetables. Halloween, which 'does not correspond to our *Art*', is again mentioned; the event ended with the 'well-known' song, 'The Woods Are Already Bright'. Many were 'thankful for the lovely hours in harmonious community', and new members joined — all now 'properly ready for autumn thoughts and moods' (ibid.).

Fig. 6.5 Screenshot of local NPD's Facebook page, 'Protection of the environment is protection of the Heimat'. This NPD slogan (here used by the NPD youth organisation) is popular at all levels of the party, as well as among independent extremists. Source: Facebook page NPD Berlin-Pankow, http://www.facebook.com/npd.pankow/photo s/a.475618535916618.1073741827.475614375917034/851724564972678/

This is evocative, of course, of the *Heimat* idyll. We would also like to point to the function played by the *form* as well as the fact of festival reports. The narratives, although varying in tone, tend to have predictable content. The group convenes; key symbols are displayed; there is movement through space, speeches, songs, and poetry; people enjoy food, drink, and games; finally, there is a happy dispersal — upon which, often, the overriding moral is spelled out (e.g., in a concluding poem). Durkheimian scholars of ritual would consider these group rituals as a means of reinforcing community by confirming the eternal validity of its values. The posting of a website narrative of the meeting might, in its turn, do more than spread complacency and (hopefully) trigger emulative action. It might (we argue) also serve to publicly affirm the efficacy and significance of the rituals. The story itself, we postulate, reinforces communal memory; its standardised form cleanses and focuses members' social recollection. Finally, the narrative might function as a linked element in a larger collective of website texts. Future party members could take the text as a sort of *liturgy* when planning their own festivals (and their own reports on those performances).

See, they might say, these are not just random bodies bumbling about. These are patriotic Germans fighting for the survival of their species by reclaiming nature, land usages, collective practices: biomass reclaiming biotope.

For one should not forget that invocations of idyllic *Heimat* are not innocent. The above may seem an innocuous re-invention of a nature-loving, community-affirming, environmentalist Germanic tradition; but there is always a link between this idyll and the media frame of angry activism, brought together under the shared 'irreparability' narrative. Some Ring reports on seasonal rituals, indeed, openly demonstrate the marriage. Take, for instance, the 'Summer Fest and Summer Solstice in Baden-Württemberg' of 2013 (held by the party as a whole; see Ring.de: Sommerfest). The festivities included a speech, stands with traditional local as well as vegan foods, playing space for children, and 'Viking' contests for 'big and small', the latter arranged by the NPD's National Youth. A bonfire was planned, together with speeches and songs. The report includes images of group activities and symbolic ('pagan') constructions (ibid.).

Thus far, the report's tone is celebratory. But it suddenly changes to angry scorn: the police intervened. The fire was forbidden. The Summer Festival was resumed, and its various (standard, ritualised) actions detailed; but the tone remains one of embattled militancy. Participants formed a circle of lit torches, sang the *Deutschlandlied* [German national anthem], and listened to poetry; a 'fire speaker' (*Feuerredner*) assured them that each torch was 'for our *Heimat*'. 'Strengthened' by words and song, all went home 'with a good feeling, despite all repression'. The battle, it seems, would go on: 'Also next year we will again hold a Summer Solstice Festival of NPD Baden-Württemberg. *We promise this!*' (their emphasis). The narrative ends with a poem. 'Once upon a time, when the country was still free', there stood 'at Summer Solstice, on every height a fire [...] We greet the sun that stands over us. May the heart also remain bright and true that never forgets its origins'. Pro-nature rituals (including vegan food-stands) combine, here, with nationalist militancy (ibid.).

From women singing autumn songs to fire-speakers, police, and *Deutschlandlied*: the pro-nature performance narratives are shifting from the timeless and idyllic to the urgent, angry-fearful media frame.

Unsurprisingly, this is clearly illustrated by pro-nature performance narratives posted by the NPD's National-Democratic Youth (Junge Nationaldemokraten, JN; the website tag is Aktion-Widerstand.de). In 2013, this group numbered around 350 members; it was affiliated with the NPD, but also termed itself 'national-revolutionary' in the 'proto-political field'. This involved links to the loosely organised, informal nationalist groups and gangs — e.g., Freie Kräfte and Autonome Nationalisten — whose group identity often depended on neighbourhood, music, street performance, and violence. These are the groups that are often responsible for illegal direct action (*Verfassungsschutzbericht* 2012, 99).

The homepage of 'Youth for Germany' uses the NPD colour-scheme, but features, as background, a fertile farming landscape. The 'Our Goals' heading mentions 'a German-European principle of lineage and descent [*Abstammungsprinzip*]', that is, biomass. As usual, territory and culture interact: 'We want our culture to live and be preserved. Therefore, we support the traditions of our thousands-year-old culture, which is so closely bound to the land in which we live' (AW.de: Ziele).

Given this, the JN do engage in the party's pro-nature, seasonal festivals. In 2013, the website gave the Germanic origins of Walpurgis Night and urged comrades to enjoy celebrating it. For Easter 2013, coffee, cakes, and games united comrades in an 'ur-Germanic festival'. 'Come to us, you also, and be who you are — youth, forward!' The youth of Lausitzmarsch have gone on a nature-hike and celebrated the summer solstice. 'With songs, poems, fire-speeches, torches, flags, and a small fire we carried on the tradition of our people. All in all, it was a deep experience in the community' (AW.de: Walpurgis; Ostern; Lausitz).

Furthermore, the JN website provides many accounts of nature-hikes, ranging from one-day affairs for the whole family to all-male marches: 'Lived Community', the New Year 'Through Forest and Sand for Fatherland', 'To Hike Always Gives Fresh Air' (featuring the poem 'Kameradschaft is Stronger Than Death') (AW.de: Gemeinschaft; Wald und Sand; Luft). A comrade's post explains the ideology supposedly underlying these hikes.

> What are we then looking for? We want to live close to nature, do not need the luxury that is supposedly so important in our lives [...] In our hearts burns the longing for freedom. This we no longer find in the dirty

streets of our towns [...] We storm [*stürmen*] to the countryside [...] We long to feel our own earth [under our feet], get to know our own *Heimat*. To see and experience how great our Germany is. We wish to experience true community. (AW.de: Warum)

The hikes and their associated camps (Autumn Camp, New Year's Camp, Pentecost Bund Camp) are meant to give youth an experience of the 'greatness of Germany', to feel their *Heimat*'s 'own earth' under their feet, to 'experience true community', to 'be who you [really] are' (ibid.). They probably promote comradeship and enthuse younger members by combining shared bodily movement, song, and food with isolation from everyday society. This, at least, is how the nature-hike narratives on the JN website present the experience.

The tone of nature-hike narratives vacillates, interestingly, between the angry activist and the happy idyll. The report on New Year's Eve hike of 'JN Mecklenburg' along the Baltic coast's 'native' woods and beaches is more grim than happy. The hike was used to 'exchange thoughts about the political battle and also to get to know still unknown co-fighters better personally'. While the 'typical BRD youth' can 'scarcely wait for the drunkenness of New Year's Eve', the report concludes, the hikers 'dedicate themselves to the *Gemeinschaft* [community] while keeping spirits and bodies sound' (AW.de: Wald und Sand).

Other narratives are a combination of activism and idyll. The report on a Christmas Day 'Hike in Rothaargebirge' describes a dozen JN members in a 'mountain landscape characterised by the woods, fields, and rivers'. Once there, they erected tents and flag, and took off through the woods 'with *Volkstreuen* songs on their lips'. They supposedly impressed other hikers, who were surprised that there were 'nationalists' like this. The young men bathed in the river, listened to bird songs, engaged in communal sports and lessons in self-defence, ate, drank, slept, cleaned up the campsite, and returned home — a fine combination of being friendly to nature, advertising the party, and training as activists (AW.de: Rothaargebirge).

Some reports, finally, make the enjoyment of an idyll into an activist act. The 2012 account of the annual mixed-sex 'JN Easter March' exults in the exploration of Germany's natural-cultural landscape. After visiting the ruins of the 'impregnable fortress Hohentwiel', young people 'snatched up their banners' and marched through 'several small villages, which we greeted, loudly, with marching songs'. Setting up camp, they 'enjoyed the lovely nature' by eating, singing, and playing games around the fire. All these activities were part of 'this beautiful hike full of fun and community in this special landscape. Do you also want to be a part of this community and take part in one of our numerous hikes? Then sign up at the following address' (AW.de: Vulkane).

The tone in this last account is fairly bucolic; like the other hike reports, it shows how enjoyment of the German idyll makes for sound bodies, creates community, *and* reconnects hikers with the identity-affirming nature of the German *Heimat*. For the JN, moreover, the idyll is never far from activism; recreation in nature has an ultimate, soldierly purpose. Indeed, enjoyment of nature is itself an activist act. The singing *Rothaargebirge* hikers impressed other nature-lovers; the Easter youths traversed villages, carrying banners and 'loudly' singing marching songs (of, one suspects, a patriotic bent). This German *Heimat* is free of alien biomass, foreigners, plants or animals, buildings or cultural practices. Indeed, the landscape is now re-inscribed with German consciousness through the songs and banners, the sound, pure bodies of militantly German youth.

German biomass is thus itself a weapon, as the JN insert *their* clean bodies, *their* concern for nature directly into threatened spaces. In 2012–2013, they were, for instance, proud participants in so-called 'Social Days', initiated (according to the NPD's website) to

> make a contribution to the community [...] cleaning public places and monuments, [providing] food for the needy, visiting children's and old people's homes, holding children's festivals, and much more [...] Germany is not only an economic location, but also *Heimat* and Fatherland. It is up to us alone to preserve a beautiful country. (npd.de: Sozialer Tag)

Some JN groups use Social Days for political demonstrations; others dedicate the time to ostentatiously cleaning up natural spaces. Thus in Niedersachsen, as the local NPD website post ('Together for a Cleaner Environment') tells us, 'eager *Heimat*-true activists' from the JN took part in the battle against 'the dirtying of the environment'. They cleaned up a recreational roadside area, finding half-empty vodka bottles and marijuana cigarette butts — the 'participating activists were, on occasion, very startled'. Many people evidently do not care where they litter. 'This tendency towards egoism has its roots, quite naturally, in the liberal-capitalist system, which must be overcome. The JN will also in the future engage itself in social encounters among our *Volk*!' (npd. niedersachsen.de: Gemeinsam).

Just under that item, one finds 'Social Day of the NPD: JN In Bremen Too'. Here, the youth clean up park playgrounds. The vodka-bottles, cigarette-packages, and heroin-needles they find provide a cross-section of the German Republic's addiction-society (*Suchtgesellschaft*), we are told. Further, the fact that 'German children' are a 'minority' in many Bremen playgrounds 'not infrequently leads to problems'. 'In connection with the cleansing of playgrounds', the surrounding households got JN leaflets in their mailboxes (npd-niedersachsen.de: Sozialer Tag).

From nature and parkland playgrounds to society itself: Germany should be kept clean. German youth, drawing mind-and-body strength from the natural, healthy, environmentalist idyll of the *Heimat*, are ready to go to angry war with those that threaten that environment and, thus, the entire German *Volk*. The two media frames, idyll and anger, meet in his — and, sometimes, her — pure German biomass.

One can, finally, argue that these three interconnected levels of media manage, together, to achieve something in an area where many other environmentalist movements fail — including many on the liberal left. They integrate nature into the human condition: biomass into biotope. Nature is *not* just a resource to exploit. It is essential to race consciousness: one would, supposedly, be as lost without the nature of one's *Heimat* as one would be without its culture, history, or human biomass. People and countryside are connected; all are native biomass. This connection, so constructed, is perhaps more deeply ecocritical than the liberal tropes of 'sustainable development'. It is also frightening.

References

Berstain, Carlos, Paez, Darío and González, José Luis, 'Rituals, Social Sharing, Silence, Emotions and Collective Memory Claims', *Psicothema*, 12 (2000), 117–130.

Blickle, Peter, *Heimat — A Critical Theory of the German Idea of Homeland* (New York: Candem House, 2004).

Brandstetter, Marc, *Die 'neue' NPD: Zwischen Systemfeindschaft und bürgerlicher Fassade* (Bonn: Konrad-Adenauer-Stiftung, 2012).

Brüggemeier, Franz-Josef, Cioc, Mark and Zeller, Thomas, eds., *How Green Were the Nazis?: Nature, Environment, and Nation in the Third Reich* (Athens, OH: Ohio University Press, 2006).

Cox, Robert, *Environmental Communication and the Public Sphere* (Los Angeles, London and New Delhi: Sage, 2013).

Crang, Michael, 'Cultural Regions and their Uses: the Interpretation of Landscape and Identity', in *Cultural Regions and Regional Cultures*, ed. by Gilberto Gimenez (Quereterao: 1st Conaculta Conference on Regional Cultures, 2003), pp. 26–34.

Deutscher Bundestag (Deutscher Bundestag Drucksache 17/9785), *Mögliche Aktivitäten von Mitgliedern der verbotenen Heimattreuen Deutschen Jugend innerhalb der Jungen Nationaldemokraten*, http://dip21.bundestag.de/dip21/btd/17/097/1709785.pdf

Ditt, Karl, 'The Idea of German Cultural Regions in the Third Reich: The Work of Franz Petri', *Journal of Historical Geography*, 27(2) (2001), 241–258, http://dx.doi.org/10.1006/jhge.2001.0298

Dominick, Raymond, *The Environmental Movement in Germany: Prophets and Pioneers, 1871–1971* (Bloomington: Indiana University Press, 1992).

Ecker, Gisela, *Kein Land in Sicht: Heimat — Weiblich?* (München: Fink Verlag, 1997).

Haverbeck, Werner Georg, 'Ökologie und Nation: Die Grundlegungen des ökologischen Bewusstseins in Deutschland', in *Handbuch zur Deutschen Nation*, ed. by Bernard Willms (Tübingen: Hohenrain, 1987), pp. 397–431.

Jost, Hermand, *Grüne Utopien in Deutschland: Zur Geschichte des ökologischen Bewußtseins* (Frankfurt: Fischer Taschenbuch Verlag, 1991).

Manning, Kathleen, *Rituals, Ceremonies, and Cultural Meaning in Higher Education* (Westport: JF Bergin & Garvey, 2000).

Markham, William, *Environmental Organizations in Modern Germany: Hardy Survivors in the Twentieth Century and Beyond* (New York: Berghahn Books, 2008).

Najoks, Claudia, 'Grün oder braun? Zum nationalistischen Ökomagazin "Umwelt und Aktiv"', *Zeit Online* (29/8/2008), http://blog.zeit.de/stoerungsmelder/2008/08/29/grun-oder-braun-zum-nationalistischen-okomagazin-%E2%80%9Eumwelt-und-aktiv%E2%80%9C_387

N.N., 'Polizei geht gegen NPD-Jugendorganisation vor', *NDR online* (21/12/2012), http://www.ndr.de/der_ndr/presse/mitteilungen/pressemeldungndr7393.html

—, 'Der Bundesvorstand der NPD', *Recherche Nord*, http://www.recherche-nord.com/article/JN_Bundesvorstand/

Olsen, Jonathan, *Nature and Nationalism: Right-Wing Ecology and the Politics of Identity in Contemporary Germany* (London: Palgrave Macmillan, 1990).

Páez, Dari, Basabe, Nekane and Gonzales, Jose Luis, 'Social Processes and Collective Memory', in *Collective Memory of Political Events*, ed. by James W. Pennebaker, Dario Páez and Bernard Rimé (Mahway: Lawrence Ehrlbaum 1997), pp. 147–174.

Pfaffinger, Christian, 'Neonazi-Strategie: Braune Bio-Kameradschaft', *Spiegel Online* (3/4/2012), http://www.spiegel.de/politik/deutschland/rechtsextreme-entdecken-den-umweltschutz-a-814893.html

Sharma, Mukul, *Green and Saffron: Hindu Nationalism and Indian Environmental Politics* (Ranikhet Cantt, India: Orient Blackswan, 2012).

Staud, Toraluf, 'Rechte Grüne, Wie Rechte in der Ökoszene mitmischen', in *Braune Ökologen, Hintergründe und Strukturen am Beispiel Mecklenburg-Vorpommerns* (Heinrich Böll Stiftung: Rostock, 2012), pp. 14–17, https://www.boell.de/sites/default/files/Braune-Oekologen.pdf

Valjent, Alina, 'Braun statt Grün: Das vermeintliche Ökomagazin "Umwelt & Aktiv"', http://www.netz-gegen-nazis.de/artikel/umwelt-aktiv-7998

Verfassungsschutzbericht 2012, Bundesministerium des Inneren, http://www.verfassungsschutz.de/embed/vsbericht-2012.pdf

Verfassungsschutzbericht 2011, Bundesministerium des Inneren, http://www.bmi.bund.de/SharedDocs/Downloads/DE/Broschueren/2012/vsb2011.pdf?__blob=publicationFile

On-Line Resources

NPD

http://www.npd.de/themen

http://www.npd.de/oftgefragt

http://www.npd.de/geschichte

http://www.npd-materialdienst.de

http://www.npd.de/thema/umwelt

http://www.facebook.com/npd.de

Meldungen Nov/Dec 2013:

http://www.npd.de/import-von-kriminellen-auslaendern-endlich-stoppen

http://www.npd.de/gegen-die-verramschung-der-staatsbuergerschaft-und-die-abwicklung-des-deutschen-volkes

http://www.npd.de/asylbewerber-koennten-schwere-erkrankungen-nach-deutschland-bringen

Meldungen Dec 2015-Jan 2016 (Kurzmeldungen with Facebook links):

https://npd.de/kuschelpolitik-beenden-kriminelle-auslaender-abschieben

https://npd.de/die-bundeswehr-muss-deutschland-auch-im-inland-verteidigen-duerfen

https://npd.de/rechtsstaatlichkeit-statt-integrationsunsinn

https://npd.de/die-mehrheit-der-deutschen-sieht-in-der-zuwanderung-keine-bereicherung

https://npd.de/am-09-01-auf-nach-koeln-deutsche-frauen-sind-kein-freiwild

https://www.facebook.com/npd.de/posts/10153611942464584:0

https://www.facebook.com/npd.de/photos/a.299179259583.146986.268232929583/10153613615799584/?type=3&theater

Recht auf *Heimat*: http://npd.de/inhalte/daten/dateiablage/Themen*Heimat*_2010.pdf

Kondome, https://npd.de/kondome-fuer-auslaender-und-ausgewaehlte-deutsche

Sozialer Tag, http://www.facebook.com/npd.de/posts/352125561563995

Pilze, http://www.facebook.com/npdmup/posts/662393643783821

NPD Bayern

Völkerschützer, http://www.npd-bayern.de/index.php/menue/24/thema/69/id/1795/anzeigemonat/05/akat/1/anzeigejahr/2008/infotext/Werden_Sie_Voelkerschuetzer/Aktuelles.html

Meldungen 2011:

http://www.npd-bayern.de/index.php/menue/24/thema/69/id/2922/
anzeigemonat/05/akat/1/anzeigejahr/2011/infotext/Tuerkenfahnen_ueber_
Wuerzburg/Aktuelles.html

http://www.npd-bayern.de/index.php/menue/24/thema/69/id/2990/
anzeigemonat/07/akat/1/anzeigejahr/2011/infotext/Winterolympiade_nicht_
in_Muenchen/Aktuelles.html

http://www.npd-bayern.de/index.php/menue/24/thema/69/id/3025/
anzeigemonat/07/akat/1/anzeigejahr/2011/infotext/Die_deutschen_
Milchbauern_ein_aussterbender_Berufsstand/Aktuelles.html

http://www.npd-bayern.de/index.php/menue/24/thema/69/id/3022/
anzeigemonat/07/akat/1/anzeigejahr/2011/infotext/Millionenfache_
Tierquaelerei_erlaubt/Aktuelles.html

Intakte Natur, http://www.npd-bayern.de/index.php/menue/24/thema/69/
id/258/anzeigemonat/09/anzeigejahr/2008/infotext/Eine_intakte_Natur_ist_
Grundlage_unserer_Zukunft/akat/1/such_0/intakte/such_1/natur/Aktuelles.
html. See duplicate at http://www.umweltundaktiv.de/Heimatschutz/
Heimatschutz-was-ist-das

NPD Niedersachsen

Sozialer Tag, http://www.npd-niedersachsen.de/index.php/menue/24/
thema/2462/id/3494/akat/3/infotext/Sozialer_von_NPD_JN_auch_in_
Bremen/Junge_Nationaldemokraten.html

Gemeinsam, http://www.npd-niedersachsen.de/index.php/menue/24/
thema/2462/id/3499/akat/3/infotext/Gemeinsam_fuer_eine_saubere_
Umwelt/Junge_Nationaldemokraten.html

Junge Nationale: Aktion-Widerstand.de

Ziele, http://www.aktion-widerstand.de/?page_id=6117

Walpurgis, http://www.aktion-widerstand.de/?p=8477

Lausitz, http://www.aktion-widerstand.de/?p=8927

Ostern, http://www.aktion-widerstand.de/?p=8242

Warum, http://www.aktion-widerstand.de/?p=5711

Gemeinschaft, http://www.aktion-widerstand.de/?p=9435

Wald und Sand, http://www.aktion-widerstand.de/?p=5398

Luft, http://www.aktion-widerstand.de/?p=4004

Vulkane, http://www.aktion-widerstand.de/?p=5544

Rothaargebirge, http://www.aktion-widerstand.de/?p=9613

Ring Nationaler Frauen

Advent, http://www.ring-nationaler-frauen-deutschland.de/index.php/meldungen/341-thueringer-advents-aktion

Orchid, http://www.ring-nationaler-frauen-deutschland.de/index.php/meldungen/134-besuch-bei-den-heimischen-orchideen

Brauchtum, http://www.ring-nationaler-frauen-deutschland.de/index.php/brauchtum-und-kultur

Mariae, http://www.ring-nationaler-frauen-deutschland.de/index.php/brauchtum-und-kultur/74-mariae-himmelfahrt-und-das-kraeuterbueschel

Sommer, http://www.ring-nationaler-frauen-deutschland.de/index.php/brauchtum-und-kultur/77-sommersonnenwende

Fasching, http://www.ring-nationaler-frauen-deutschland.de/index.php/meldungen/191-brauchtum-zur-faschingszeit

Herbst, http://www.ring-nationaler-frauen-deutschland.de/index.php/meldungen/331-herbst-erntedank-oder-halloween

Erntedankfeier, http://www.ring-nationaler-frauen-deutschland.de/index.php/meldungen/332-erntedankfeier-in-baden-wuerttemberg

Sommerfest, http://www.ring-nationaler-frauen-deutschland.de/index.php/meldungen/137-sommerfest-und-sonnenwende-in-baden-wuerttemberg

Umwelt & Aktiv

Wir über uns, http://www.umweltundaktiv.de/presse/wir-uber-uns/wir-uber-uns

Heimatschutz, http://www.umweltundaktiv.de/Heimatschutz/die-ur-bevoelkerung-europas-eine-laengst-faellige-richtigstellung

Other websites

http://www.nsantispe.wordpress.com

Umwelt & Aktiv: articles cited

2009, 2: Sojka, Klaus, 'Tierschutz und Kirchen'.

2010, 2: Kast, D., 'Hermann Löns: Heidedichter, Naturschützer und ungehörter Warner'; Anon., 'Baum des Jahres 2010'; Anon., 'Aromatherapie'; Anon., 'Die Kräuterhexe'; 'Wie gefährlich ist Werbung nun wirklich?'; Blum, Robert, 'Schiefergas: Energiepolitik zwischen Autarkie und Grundwasservergiftung'; Anon., 'Genmanipulierte Erdnussbutterkekse'; Anon., 'Kängurufleisch — Tierquälerei vom anderen Ende der Welt'.

2010, 4: Fürst, Alexander, 'Der germanischen Julfest'; B.A.H., 'Tierische Einwanderer'.

2011, 1: Howanietz, Michael, 'Sol invictus'; Howanietz, Michael, 'Der genormte Mensch'; Anon., 'Dialog zwischen zweit Samen Geni och Normi'; Ulrich Dittmann, 'Tierrechte'.

2011, 2: Blum, Robert, 'Klonfleisch von US-Farmen: United States of Klonfleisch: Klonfleisch auf deutschen Tellern'; Horn, Laura, 'Asiatische Maikäfer'; Weber, Britta, 'Mama Afrika — der geknechtete Kontinent: Schnelleres globales Bevölkerungswachstum'.

2011, 3: Blum, Robert, 'Deutschland stirbt'.

2011, 4: Dittmann, Ulrich, 'Tierschutzberichte der Bundesregierung von 2011 — ein Dokument des Versagens'; Thüne, Wolfgang, 'Landwirtschaft — Klimaschutz frisch vom Acker?'; Mireille, Dankwart (film review).

2012, 2: Zittmayr, Renate, 'Gentechnik-freies Österreich'.

Index

activist media. *See* media
Adams, Michael 79, 90
Alia, Valerie 82
Altheide, David L. 5, 6, 65, 81
Amazon region 83, 86, 93, 96
Anderson, Alison 77, 92
Anthropocene 80
Antifaschistische Aktion 142
anxiety rhetoric. *See* rhetoric
Arctic 76
Argentina 7, 8, 12, 22–25, 36, 48
Asamblea Ciudadana Ambiental de
    Gualeguayú (ACAG) 25, 28, 31,
    34, 36, 37, 39, 41–45
Atkinson, Joshua 26
authority 65
Avison, Shannon 76, 82
Ayers, Michael 26

Bailey, Olga 26
Bauman, Zygmunt 123
Bennett, W. Lance 9, 26
Beowulf Mining 56, 57, 61
Berglez, Peter 85
Bimber, Bruce 27
biodiversity 9, 86, 113, 117, 122, 126,
    128, 130, 131, 132
blogs 105–107, 109, 111, 116, 119, 124,
    129–132
  blogosphere 13, 40, 105, 107–113,
    117, 118, 120, 122, 123, 127, 129,
    130, 131

Bonner, Frances 115, 119
Boykoff, Jules M. 6
Boykoff, Maxwell T. 6, 80
Brazil 23–25, 36
Bredin, Marian 77, 82
Bruns, Axel 54
Bryman, Alan 84

Canada 36, 77, 83, 84, 90, 92, 94, 95
Canadian Broadcasting Corporation
    (CBC) 94
Carbaugh, Donal 3
Carrol, William C. 26
Castells, Manuel 21, 37, 44, 45
Chile 23, 24, 36
'Chilean Winter' 23
Clarkson, Linda 79
climate 75–81, 83–85, 87, 89–92,
    94–100
Confederation of the Indigenous
    Nationalities of the Ecuadorian
    Amazon (CONFENIAE) 83, 86
connectivity 23, 24, 110, 116, 130
  connective communication 113, 124
consumption 54, 70, 105, 115, 116,
    117, 119–124, 130, 131, 147, 154
conversation 39, 123
  public debate 41
Corbett, Julia 15, 117
Cox, Robert 1, 6, 7, 145
Coyer, Kate 26

Dagens Nyheter 68
Dean, Jodi 54
de Chavez, Raymond 83, 90, 96, 97
de Jong, Wilma 26
Deuze, Mark 5, 81, 99
disturbance 1, 2, 70, 108, 125
Downing, John 26, 34

Ebba Grön 59, 60, 67
ecocritics 4, 146–148
ecology
    media 10, 11, 77, 78, 81, 82, 85, 91,
        94, 95, 96, 97, 98, 99
    natural 75, 78, 81, 85, 97, 99, 100
ecosystem 21, 75, 76, 79, 83, 84, 86, 88,
    89, 90, 124
emotions (feelings) 5, 14, 39, 80, 81,
    113, 114, 117, 123, 124, 125, 126,
    140, 145, 156
Empresa Nacional de Celulosa
    España (Ence) 25, 36
engagement 8, 22, 26, 34, 35, 37, 39,
    40, 42, 44, 45, 46, 47, 154
Entman, Robert 5, 11
environmental activism 36, 53, 56, 67
environmentalism 13, 137, 140, 145,
    149, 154
Eriksen, Christine 79
Evernden, Lorne Leslie Neil 55

Facebook 25, 28, 42, 45, 46, 53, 57, 59,
    69, 71, 96, 142, 143, 159, 167
Fairclough, Norman 29
fear rhetoric. *See* rhetoric
Finland 36, 55, 76
Flanagin, Andrew 27
Foust, Christina R. 6, 108
Fox, Elizabeth 21
Fuchs, C. 54, 109

Gállok Region 55–59, 61, 62, 64, 65, 71
gardening 8, 9, 13, 14, 105, 106, 110,
    113–134, 154
Germany 8, 106, 138, 141, 142, 144,
    145, 150, 152, 156, 161–166
globalisation 32, 55, 138, 147, 151

Graf, Heike 1, 8, 9, 10, 13, 105, 109,
    110, 113, 114, 116, 119, 123, 127,
    132
Grupo Guayubira 25, 31, 35, 41, 44,
    45, 46
Gurak, Laura 106

Hackett, Robert A. 26
Hafsteinsson, Sigurjón Baldur 77, 82
Haider, Jutta 107
Hallin, Daniel 21
Hall, Stuart 2
Hammarskjöld, Dag 58
Hansen, Andreas 2, 5, 6, 7
Heimat 14, 15, 139, 142–150, 152, 154,
    157, 159–165, 167
Hellmann, Kai-Uwe 123, 124
Hjarvard, Stig 14, 66
Hulme, Mike 80, 99
human-nature relationship 3–7, 54,
    70, 71, 75, 80, 86, 87, 99, 119, 121,
    151, 155
Huntington, Henry 80

indigenous people
    approaches 87
    media 77, 78, 95–99
    rights 54, 55, 65, 69, 83
information 1, 6, 8, 10, 11, 13, 22, 24,
    26, 27, 30, 33–36, 38, 42, 43, 44, 46,
    48, 57, 58, 59, 63, 65, 66, 69, 70, 71,
    81, 82, 96, 97, 107–111, 113, 115,
    121, 128, 132, 141, 145, 151, 157
International Court of Justice 25
Internet 9, 10, 22, 23, 24, 26, 27, 34, 36,
    37, 38, 42–51, 56, 70, 96, 106, 116
Inuit Youth Delegation 83, 88, 92, 93,
    94
irritation. *See* resonance

Janus, Noreene 21
Jenkins, Henry 9
Jørgensen, Finn Arne 70

Kenix, Linda Jean 27
Konek, Curtis 83, 89, 95

Konek, Jordan 83, 94, 95
Kurvits, Tina 83, 90–92, 94

Labov, William 5, 67
Larsen, Vibeke 83, 84, 89, 98
Latour, Bruno 2, 5
Layton, Matthew 23
Leistert, Oliver 27
Leivrouw, Leah 26
Lester, Libby 6
Logan, Robert K. 81, 82
Lopez, Lori Kido 106
Luhmann, Niklas 1–5, 7, 8, 15, 16, 108, 110, 111, 112, 113, 131
Lundberg Tuorda, Tor 60, 65

MacCaughey, Martha 26
Many Strong Voices 83, 84, 90, 91
Märak, Mimie 57
marginalisation 9, 54, 65–66, 76, 96
Maturana, Humberto R. 3
McGregor, Deborah 79, 80
McKay, George 114
McLuhan, Marshall 81
Meadows, Michael 77, 82
media
  activist 67
  alternative 77
  coverage 6, 22, 24, 48, 76, 77, 84, 91, 96, 98
  digital 8, 22, 23, 24, 26, 28, 42, 43, 44, 46, 47, 48
  indigenous. *See* indigenous people
  logic 5, 10, 14, 65, 67, 70, 71, 98, 143, 144, 145
  mainstream 6, 9, 10, 12, 14, 21, 24, 26, 30, 33, 34, 35, 44, 46, 47, 48, 75, 76, 77, 78, 82, 83, 84, 91, 92, 94, 95, 96, 97, 98, 99, 141, 150, 158
  national 48, 65, 77, 94, 95, 100
  participatory 10, 53, 54, 56, 68, 70, 71, 85
  practice 27, 28, 92
  theories 2, 3, 14, 78
mediatisation 14, 66

Melián, Virginia 8, 21, 27
Merchant, Carolyn 121
Metsä-Botnia 24, 25, 31, 36
Milstein, Tema 119
mining 8, 11, 12, 15, 53, 53–65, 67–71
mobilisation 22–24, 27, 28, 36, 37, 42, 44, 45, 47, 48, 55
monoculture 22, 23, 30, 36, 40, 47, 48
Morozov, Eugene 27
Morrissette, Vern 79
Moseley, Mason 23

narratives 9, 28, 63, 64, 65, 67, 71, 137, 138, 141, 143–145, 151, 155, 157–160
National-Democratic Party of Germany (NPD) 138–150, 152–154, 156, 157, 159–161, 163–168
nature 1, 3–7, 9, 12, 14, 15, 32, 53–56, 58–66, 70, 71, 76, 79, 80, 82, 83, 86, 87, 88, 91, 99, 100, 108, 116, 117, 119, 120, 121, 126, 132, 146–158, 160–164
  natural resources 9, 14, 21, 22, 31, 53, 61, 63, 70, 71, 79, 86, 119, 124, 132
neo-Nazi 8, 137, 138, 140, 145, 154, 156, 157
networking. *See* Social Networks
news media 5–7, 13–15, 30, 33, 34, 48, 75, 79, 82, 83, 85, 91, 92, 94, 95, 98, 108, 131
  news values 10, 12, 14
non-human environment 1–7, 11, 14, 15, 16, 108, 112, 113, 116, 123, 132
Norway 55, 76, 83, 84, 89, 95, 96
Nye, David E. 55
Nystrom, Christine 81

observation 3, 6, 15, 29, 85, 109, 121
  observer 2, 4, 5, 108, 109, 111, 113
Olausson, Ulrika 6, 85
Olin-Scheller, Christina 54
online platforms 29
O'Shannon Murphy, William 6

Pakkasvirta, Jussi 22
Papathanassopoulos, Stylianos 21
Paulette, François 83, 84, 90, 95, 96, 98
Peruzzoti, Enrique 22
Pezullio, Phaedra C. 7
Pietikäinen, Sari 77, 82
polarisation of debate 69
Pole, Antoinette 106, 155
Postman, Neil 81
power 15, 29, 31, 54, 55, 60, 65, 67, 76,
   85, 96, 98, 118, 151, 153, 154
protest 8, 10, 11, 15, 22–28, 31–42,
   44–48, 55, 60, 63, 138
Puanchir, Tito 83, 86, 87, 93, 96, 97
pulp mills 7, 10, 12, 22–25, 30, 31, 33,
   35, 36, 40, 48

REDES Amigos de la Tierra 25, 31,
   36, 41, 43, 44, 45
Regallet, Gabriel 79
representation 32, 71, 84
   media frames 7, 15, 16, 30, 31, 47,
      59, 63, 69, 137, 145, 146, 150, 156,
      160
   resonance 5–8, 11, 15, 67, 107, 108,
      112, 130, 131, 145
   rhetoric 6, 7, 13, 113, 114, 131, 140,
      142
      anxiety 14
      fear 6, 7, 13, 14, 15, 16, 137, 140,
         143, 144, 145, 149
Robertson, Carmen L. 77
Rockwell, Rick 21
Rodríguez, Clemencia 26
Roosvall, Anna 8, 9, 10, 12, 75–78, 80,
   82, 83, 84, 86, 89, 92, 97
Russell, Adrienne 77, 82
Russia 55, 76, 84
Rydberg, Tomas 55

Sámi 76, 79, 83, 84, 87, 89, 96
Sassen, Saskia 54
Schmidt, Jan 106, 107, 112
Schutz, Alfred 3, 4

Segerberg, Alexandra 9, 26, 28
Siles, Ignacio 106
Sinclair-Poulton, Clive 56–57
social movements 34, 44, 156
social networks 95
   networking 27, 29, 34, 83, 94, 105,
      107, 109, 112, 122, 123, 124, 130,
      132
South Africa 79, 83
Stein, Laura 27, 28
Stohl, Cynthia 27
sustainability 9, 58, 59, 63, 70, 83, 108,
   113, 115, 119, 127, 128, 131, 146
Suzuki, David 80
Sweden 8, 53, 55, 57, 67, 76, 77, 79, 95
Swedish Environmental Code 58,
   59, 66

Tam, Kim-Pong 60
Tauli-Corpuz, Victoria 76, 80, 81
Taylor, Lisa 114, 115
Tebtebba 76, 83, 84, 90, 96
Tegelberg, Matthew 8, 9, 10, 75, 76,
   77, 78, 82, 83, 84, 86, 89, 92, 93, 97
Tipa, Gail 80
Tracy, Christine 82
Traditional Ecological Knowledge
   (TEK) 10, 11, 14, 75, 78–82, 85–91,
   97, 99
Treré, Emiliano 26
Twitter 25, 28, 42, 45, 53, 71, 95, 96,
   98, 140, 142

Umwelt & Aktiv 149–155, 170
United Nations (UN) 76, 79, 90
Uruguay 7, 8, 11, 12, 22–25, 30–33, 36,
   40, 48

Van de Donk, Wim 26
Varela, Francisco J. 3
visuals 137, 138, 140
   visuality 113
Volk 139, 141–144, 143, 144, 147–152,
   148, 149, 150, 151, 152, 164
Von Foerster, Heinz 3

Waisbord, Silvio 21, 22
Waletzky, Joshua 5, 67
Waters, Richard D. 27
websites 10, 34, 41, 42, 56, 57, 95, 111, 143–153, 157–163
Welp, Yanina 22, 23
Wheatly, Jonathan 22

Wikström, Patrik 54
wildlife 59, 91

YouTube 11, 12, 25, 53, 56, 57, 60, 65, 66, 68–71, 95, 98, 140
Yulsman, Tom 80

This book need not end here...

At Open Book Publishers, we are changing the nature of the traditional academic book. The title you have just read will not be left on a library shelf, but will be accessed online by hundreds of readers each month across the globe. OBP publishes only the best academic work: each title passes through a rigorous peer-review process. We make all our books free to read online so that students, researchers and members of the public who can't afford a printed edition will have access to the same ideas.
This book and additional content is available at:
https://www.openbookpublishers.com/isbn/9781783742431

Customise

Personalise your copy of this book or design new books using OBP and third-party material. Take chapters or whole books from our published list and make a special edition, a new anthology or an illuminating coursepack. Each customised edition will be produced as a paperback and a downloadable PDF. Find out more at:
https://www.openbookpublishers.com/section/59/1

Donate

If you enjoyed this book, and feel that research like this should be available to all readers, regardless of their income, please think about donating to us. We do not operate for profit and all donations, as with all other revenue we generate, will be used to finance new Open Access publications:
https://www.openbookpublishers.com/section/13/1/support-us

Like Open Book Publishers ⬛f

Follow @OpenBookPublish 🐦

Read more at the Open Book Publishers **BLOG**

You may also be interested in:

Forests and Food: Addressing Hunger and Nutrition Across Sustainable Landscapes

Edited by Bhaskar Vira, Christoph Wildburger and Stephanie Mansourian

https://www.openbookpublishers.com/product/399

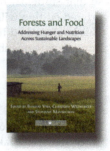

What Works in Conservation 2015

Edited by William J. Sutherland, Lynn V. Dicks, Nancy Ockendon, Rebecca K. Smith

https://www.openbookpublishers.com/product/347